# ONE-POT
## COOKING

# ONE-POT
## COOKING

*Casseroles, soups, curries, bakes
and other no-fuss family food*

## Katie Bishop

Collins

First published in 2010 by Collins

HarperCollins*Publishers*
77–85 Fulham Palace Road
London W6 8JB

www.harpercollins.co.uk

13 12 11 10
9 8 7 6 5 4 3 2 1

Photography © Dan Jones, 2010, except pages 22, 29, 108, 117, 161 and 167
Text © Katie Bishop, 2010

A catalogue record for this book is available from the British Library.

ISBN 978-0-00-732560-3

Layout by Susie Bell, www.f-12.co.uk

Colour reproduction by Dot Gradations
Printed and bound in Great Britain by Martins the Printers,
Berwick-upon-Tweed

**Mixed Sources**
Product group from well-managed
forests and other controlled sources
www.fsc.org Cert no. SW-COC-001806
© 1996 Forest Stewardship Council

FSC is a non-profit international organisation established
to promote the responsible management of the world's forests.
Products carrying the FSC label are independently certified
to assure consumers that they come from forests that are managed
to meet the social, economic and ecological needs
of present and future generations.

Find out more about HarperCollins and the environment at
**www.harpercollins.co.uk/green**

# Contents

# Introduction

I have been writing about food for almost nine years now. A lot
has changed in foodie fashion during that time, but one thing
has remained constant, I always, without fail, get asked for ideas
for simple, everyday, mid-week recipes. Recipes that are simple to
make after a hard day and use everyday ingredients that are easily
bought from the supermarket – or even the corner shop in some
cases. Quick and easy dishes that don't need hours of preparation
or complicated techniques, and don't create lots of mess. It was
with this in mind that I decided to write a set of one-pot recipes.

I hope that the following pages will be different enough to be
inspiring, but thoroughly do-able on an everyday basis. There are
recipes for family food, some for entertaining, some for comforting,
indulgent days, and others for frugal or healthy days. What they
all have in common is that they are remarkably simple to make.
It's the kind of food that I cook day to day, so I know they fit
around a busy lifestyle.

I have grouped the recipes by cooking method, rather than
ingredient. I thought that this would be easier to adapt to your
day – I don't know about you, but sometimes I just don't have time
to preheat the oven, or the inclination to wash up a large crusty
roasting tin. So on those days cooking in a pan or under the grill is
usually in order. Some days I don't even want to cook at all, which
is where the 'In a Bowl' chapter comes into its own. For other days,
when time is slightly less of an issue, there's the oven or pot for
longer, slower cooking.

Either way, I have taken 'one pot' as literally as possible. So all the recipes are cooked in one 'utensil', whether it is a casserole, pan, bowl, dish, grill pan or roasting tin. You will usually need a chopping board for each recipe, and if it benefits the recipe, I have on occasion allowed myself up to one small bowl for mixing or soaking ingredients before cooking. But my focus has most definitely been on minimising washing up and the use of equipment as much as possible. There are a couple of recipes that use two modes of cooking, where a dish is started on the hob and finished in the oven, for example, but I have purposefully kept this to a minimum to keep things as simple as possible.

Most importantly, however, I have written recipes that reflect the food that I, and my friends and family, like to eat – simple stove- or oven-to-table food that is nutritious, tasty and interesting. Most of the recipes are complete, balanced meals in themselves; others may just need a quick salad or some bread to go with it. I've also made use of the wide range of fresh noodles and cooked/microwave rice products available in supermarkets now, to make life easier. Why not! Alternatively, if you have leftover rice or noodles, these will be perfect to use in these recipes too – leftover rice needs to be cooled quickly (within an hour) and then covered and chilled immediately, for no more than 24 hours, before reheating thoroughly to limit germs forming. Never reheat rice more than once.

Each chapter has some puddings and sweet things included too, which shouldn't really constitute meals in themselves – although I'm sure there are some who would be happy if this were the case! Of course, they're all cooked or made in one pot too. The odd recipe uses raw egg white, so please be wary of this if cooking for the young, elderly or pregnant.

With simplicity comes some level of exposure. If you are making unfussy food with little faffing around, then the ingredients are very much on show. So I would always advocate using the best possible ingredients you can afford or find to maximise the results of each and every recipe. I realise that this is sometimes easier said than done and there are plenty of recipes in this book that use tins, packets or convenience products to save you time.

As with all my books, each and every recipe has been carefully tested and tweaked to make it as perfect as it can be. However, my food is ripe and ready for interpretation. So if you don't like this or that; or you fancy a bit of this, but not that; then most of my recipes will take some customisation here and there – although I can't guarantee the results if you go off spec! With the exception of the baking recipes, which in the main need to remain precise to make them work, feel free to make my recipes your own.

Either way I hope that you will enjoy every last mouthful, safe in the knowledge that there's only one pot to wash up at the end of it all!

## Cooking notes:

All the recipes in the book have been tested using metric measurements. I learnt to cook in pounds and ounces but the transition really is very easy, and I think metric measures produce more consistent, accurate results. There are conversions given throughout the book, but for consistency I would follow the metric measures every time.

All oven temperatures given are for conventional ovens. If you are using a fan oven, which tend to be rather more feisty heat wise, then I recommend dropping the temperature by about 15°C (½ Gas Mark) to achieve the same results. Check your manufacturer's instructions for more detail.

Recipes using the oven or grill are written with the assumption that they will always be fully preheated unless otherwise stated.

All spoon measurements are assumed to be level, unless stated differently. A teaspoon equates to 5ml, and a tablespoon is 15ml.

## Notes on ingredients:

You can assume that all eggs are medium sized, unless otherwise stated and free-range chicken and eggs are most definitely recommended. Happy chickens equal tasty eggs and meat.

All milk and other dairy products are full fat, unless otherwise stated. If you are vegetarian then you might want to swap conventional cheeses for vegetarian alternatives. There's a great selection available from most major supermarkets.

Cooking with extra virgin olive oil is a waste of money! Over a certain temperature the flavour and aromas that you have paid a premium for will be lost. Always cook with simple olive oil or other oil as stated in the recipe and reserve extra virgin olive oil for uncooked dishes, sauces and dressings.

I always try to give accurate weights and measures for all ingredients, but sometimes a handful of this or that is in order. As a guide you could apply the following measurements for herbs which are the most likely victims of this willy-nilly approach:

Small handful = 5g (¼oz)

Medium handful = 10g (⅓oz)

Large handful = 20g (¾oz)


**Some other helpful measurements:**

1 lemon will produce 2 teaspoons of zest and 8 tablespoons (120ml/4½oz) of juice

1 lime will produce about 1 teaspoon of zest and about 2 tablespoons (30ml/1fl oz) of juice

1 orange will produce about 1 tablespoon of zest and about 10 tablespoons (150ml/5fl oz) of juice

1 level tablespoon of finely grated Parmesan cheese = about 5g (¼oz)

5cm (2in) piece of fresh root ginger = 25g (1oz)

# In a Pot

# Aubergine and tomato curry (v.)

This curry is so quick and easy to make. It's a relatively dry curry, not swimming in sauce, and it's great as a vegetarian main or as a side dish. It also freezes well, so make a big batch and then freeze in portions.

**Preparation time:**
10 minutes

**Cooking time:**
18–22 minutes,
  plus standing

**Serves 2 as main course, 4 as a side**

4 tbsp vegetable oil
700g (1lb 9oz) aubergines
  (about 3 medium),
  trimmed and cut into
  large chunks
3 garlic cloves, peeled
  and finely grated
3–4cm (1¼–1½in) piece
  freash root ginger, peeled
  and finely grated
1 large green chilli, finely
  diced (remove the seeds if
  you prefer a milder dish)
2 tsp fennel seeds
1 tsp cumin seeds
1 tbsp ground coriander
½ tsp turmeric
1 x 400g tin chopped
  tomatoes
Sea salt and freshly
  ground black pepper
1 tbsp each chopped fresh
  coriander and mint
  leaves

**To serve**
Natural yoghurt
Warm Indian breads

Warm the vegetable oil in a large deep frying pan or wok over a high heat. Add the aubergine and stir-fry for 3–4 minutes until softened and well browned.

Add the garlic, ginger, chilli, fennel and cumin seeds and stir-fry for 2–3 minutes. Add the coriander and turmeric and fry a further 1 minute.

Stir in the tomatoes, 100ml (3½fl oz) cold water and a generous amount of salt (about ¼ teaspoon) and pepper. Cover and simmer for 10–12 minutes until thickened slightly and the aubergine is meltingly tender.

Remove from the heat and leave to stand with the lid on for 5 minutes. Stir in the herbs and serve with natural yoghurt to spoon over, and warmed Indian breads.

# Bacon and borlotti bean soup

**This hearty soup is packed with flavoursome ingredients and is ideal as a light main course with plenty of crusty bread.**

**Preparation time:**
10 minutes

**Cooking time:**
20 minutes

**Serves 4**

10 thin-cut rashers
   smoked streaky bacon
1 tbsp olive oil
2 leeks, trimmed and diced
1 fresh rosemary sprig
1 x 400g tin chopped
   tomatoes
2 tbsp tomato purée
1 x 400g tin borlotti beans,
   rinsed and drained
1.2 litres (2 pints) beef
   stock
75g (3oz) finely shredded
   kale or other dark leafy
   cabbage
Sea salt and freshly
   ground black pepper

**To serve**
Crusty bread

Dice all but 4 of the bacon rashers. Warm the oil in a medium soup pan over a high heat. Add all the bacon and fry for 3–4 minutes until golden and crisp. Using tongs, remove the whole rashers and set aside on kitchen paper.

Add the leeks to the pan and cook for a further 3 minutes until softened. Add the rosemary, tomatoes, tomato purée, beans and stock.

Bring to the boil, then leave to bubble away for 10 minutes until slightly reduced. Add the kale and simmer for a further 2 minutes or until wilted.

Season to taste with salt and pepper and remove the rosemary. Ladle into warmed bowls. Serve with the reserved crispy bacon rashers on the top, and crusty bread on the side.

# Braised chicken with creamy bacon, leeks and potatoes

To me, there's something forever comforting about the classic blend of chicken, bacon, leeks and cream. Here they are combined simply for best effect in this tasty dish, which is just as good for entertaining as it is for warming the soul during the week. As with all these things, start with good-quality chicken and the results will pay dividends.

**Preparation time:**
10 minutes

**Cooking time:**
1 hour

**Serves 4**

1.5kg (3lb 6oz) chicken, cut into 8 pieces
½ tbsp olive oil
Sea salt and freshly ground black pepper
25g (1oz) butter
150g (5oz) smoked streaky bacon, diced
2 leeks, trimmed and sliced
2 garlic cloves, peeled and chopped
500g (1lb 2oz) baby new potatoes, halved
250ml (9fl oz) white wine
350ml (12fl oz) chicken stock
100ml (4fl oz) double cream
3 tbsp chopped fresh tarragon

**To serve**
Green salad (optional)

Rub the chicken with a little olive oil and season with salt and pepper. Warm the remaining oil and the butter in a large casserole over a medium heat. Add the chicken and cook for 5–10 minutes or until golden. Remove from the pan and set aside.

Reduce the heat to low. Add the bacon, leeks, garlic and potatoes to the pan and cook for 5 minutes, stirring often, until soft. Stir in the wine, scraping up any bits from the base of the pan with a wooden spoon.

Return the chicken to the pan and add the stock. Bring to the boil then reduce the heat to low and simmer for 40–45 minutes, stirring occasionally until the potatoes are tender and the chicken is cooked through.

Stir in the cream and half of the tarragon. Leave to warm through for 5 minutes, then serve with the remaining tarragon sprinkled over the top. If you like a thicker sauce, remove the chicken and bring the sauce to the boil over a high heat to reduce, then serve. This dish is great with a green salad.

# Butter bean, corn and sweet potato chowder (v.)

This chowder is more of a stew than a soup and tastes great as a family meal with warmed flour tortillas or nachos for dunking.

**Preparation time:**
10 minutes

**Cooking time:**
35–40 minutes

## Serves 4

2 tbsp olive oil
1 large red chilli, deseeded
   and finely chopped
1 garlic clove, peeled
   and crushed
1 large red onion,
   peeled and diced
2 red peppers,
   deseeded and diced
½ tsp ground cumin
2 tsp paprika
2 sweet potatoes, about
   375g (13oz), peeled and
   cut into 2cm (¾in) cubes
350ml (12fl oz) vegetable
   stock
1 x 400g tin butter beans,
   rinsed and drained
1 x 200g tin sweetcorn,
   drained
A large handful of fresh
   coriander, chopped
3 tbsp soured cream,
   plus extra to serve
Sea salt and freshly
   ground black pepper

**To serve**
Warmed flour tortillas
   or nachos

Warm the olive oil in a casserole over a medium heat. Add the chilli, garlic, onion and peppers and cook, stirring often for 10 minutes until softened. Stir in the cumin and paprika.

Increase the heat to high. Mix in the sweet potatoes and stock. Bring to the boil, then reduce the heat to low, cover and cook for 20–25 minutes or until tender.

Using the back of your spoon, crush a few pieces of potato against the side of the pan and mix in to thicken the sauce.

Fold in the beans, sweetcorn and half of the coriander, followed by the soured cream. Season to taste with salt and pepper and scatter with a generous amount of coriander to serve. Great served with warmed flour tortillas or nachos on the side.

# Chicken, chorizo and chickpea stew

I sometimes like to use dry Fino sherry instead of white wine in this yummy stew. Either way it's very tasty and full of Spanish-inspired flavour.

**Preparation time:**
5–10 minutes

**Cooking time:**
1 hour

**Serves 4**

100g (4oz) chorizo, diced
8 chicken thighs, skin on
Sea salt and freshly
  ground black pepper
1 onion, peeled and diced
2 celery sticks, trimmed
  and diced
2 garlic cloves, peeled and
  chopped
2 fresh thyme sprigs
250ml (9fl oz) white wine
  or 100ml (4fl oz) dry Fino
  sherry made up to 250ml
  (9fl oz) with water
1 x 400g tin chickpeas,
  rinsed and drained
4 tbsp chopped fresh
  flat-leaf parsley

**To serve**
Salad leaves
Crusty bread

Warm a large casserole (ideally a wide shallow one that will take the chicken in a single layer) over a medium heat. Add the chorizo and cook for 2–3 minutes or until it releases its orangey oil.

Season the chicken. Add it skin side down to the pan and cook for 10 minutes until golden and becoming crispy.

Stir in the onion, celery, garlic and thyme and cook for 5 minutes or until soft. Add the wine or sherry mix, and the chickpeas and stir well.

Ensure all the chicken is skin side up. Bring to the boil, then reduce the heat to low and simmer gently for 40 minutes until the chicken is cooked through. Sprinkle with the parsley and serve with salad leaves and plenty of crusty bread to soak up the juices.

# Easy fish stew

**Mix and match the seafood you use in this yummy recipe depending on what's in season or easily available.**

**Preparation time:**
10–15 minutes
**Cooking time:**
25 minutes

**Serves 4**

3 tbsp olive oil
1 leek, trimmed and sliced
1 fennel bulb, trimmed and
  thinly sliced
1 x 400g tin chopped
  tomatoes
75ml (3fl oz) dry white wine
  or vermouth
1.2 litres (2 pints)
  good-quality fish stock
A large pinch of saffron
  strands
500g (1lb 2oz) firm white
  fish fillets, skin removed
450g (1lb) raw peeled tiger
  prawns
4 raw unpeeled tiger
  prawns (optional)
12 raw scallops, cleaned
12 live clams or mussels,
  cleaned
2 tbsp chopped fresh flat
  leaf parsley
Sea salt and freshly
  ground black pepper

**To serve**
Crusty bread
Rouille (see right)

Warm the olive oil in a casserole or large pot over a medium heat. Add the leek and fennel and cook for 5 minutes until soft and golden.

Add the tomatoes, wine or vermouth, stock and saffron to the pan. Bring to the boil, then reduce the heat to low and simmer for 15 minutes.

Cut the fish into chunks and add to the pan together with the peeled and unpeeled prawns, scallops, clams or mussels. Stir and cover. Leave to simmer for 2 minutes or until just cooked, the shellfish have opened and the fish is opaque. Throw away any unopened shells.

Stir the parsley through the stew and season to taste with salt and pepper. Ladle into bowls and top each one with a whole unpeeled prawn, if using. Serve with plenty of warm crusty bread and dollops of rouille if you wish.

## To make rouille:

Chargrill 2 red peppers until blackened. Alternatively, preheat the grill to medium, then cook the peppers under the hot grill, turning frequently, for 10 minutes or until blackened all over. Leave to cool, then deseed and peel off the skin. Put the flesh into a food processor, add 1 deseeded red chilli, 2 peeled garlic cloves and a pinch of salt and blitz until smooth. With the motor running, very slowly drizzle in enough extra virgin olive oil to reach your preferred consistency (I like to add about 4 tablespoons so that the rouille reaches the consistency of mayonnaise).

# Curried chicken with rice and coriander yoghurt

This one-pot chicken and rice dish works wonders! It's great during the week and I've also served it with excellent results when entertaining too — it's only mildly spiced so tends to suit everyone.

**Preparation time:**
10 minutes

**Cooking time:**
30 minutes

## Serves 4

4 chicken breasts, skin removed

2 tbsp mild curry powder

2 tbsp vegetable oil

1 onion, peeled and thinly sliced

2cm (¾in) piece fresh root ginger, peeled and grated

300g (11oz) basmati rice

750ml (1¼ pints) chicken stock

150g (5oz) natural yoghurt

2 tbsp chopped fresh coriander

Sea salt and freshly ground black pepper

**To serve**
Diced tomato, red onion, cucumber and parsley salad

Place the chicken and curry powder into a large freezer bag, seal the top and shake to coat evenly. Warm half the vegetable oil in a casserole over a medium heat. Add the chicken and cook for 5 minutes on each side, until golden. Set the chicken aside on a plate.

Add the remaining oil, onion and ginger to the casserole and cook over a medium heat for 5 minutes until just soft and golden. Add the rice and stir well to coat in the oil. Add the stock, increase the heat and bring to the boil.

When boiling, reduce the heat to very low. Return the chicken and any juices to the pan and cover with a tight-fitting lid. Leave to cook for 10 minutes (without peaking!), then remove the casserole from the heat and leave to stand (still without peaking!) for a further 5 minutes, until the liquid has been absorbed, and the chicken is cooked through.

Mix the yoghurt and coriander together and season to taste with salt and pepper. Serve the curry in bowls topped with spoonfuls of the coriander yogurt. I like to serve this with a salad of diced tomato, red onion, cucumber and parsley.

# Five-spiced duck with orange rice

**This all-in-one meal looks as good as it tastes, which makes it perfect for entertaining.**

**Preparation time:**
5 minutes

**Cooking time:**
1 hour 15 minutes

## Serves 4

4 duck legs
1 tbsp Chinese 5-spice
  powder
2 garlic cloves, peeled and
  crushed
2cm (¾in) piece fresh root
  ginger, peeled and finely
  chopped
300g (11oz) basmati rice
500ml (18fl oz) orange juice
2 tbsp fish sauce, plus extra
  to taste
4 tbsp sweet chilli sauce
4 spring onions, trimmed
  and finely shredded

**To serve**
Watercress salad

Place the duck into a large freezer bag with the Chinese 5-spice powder, seal the top and shake well to coat. Warm a large, shallow, heavy-based casserole (big enough to cook the duck in a single layer) over a medium heat. Add the duck, skin side down, and cook for 10 minutes or until golden and crispy. Turn them over and cook for a further 2 minutes. Remove the duck from the pan and set aside.

Spoon off all but about 1 tablespoon of the fat in the pan and set aside for another recipe (it's great for frying and roasting). Return the pan to a medium heat. Add the garlic and ginger and cook for 1 minute until softened. Stir in the rice, ensuring that all the grains are glistening with the fat.

Pour over the orange juice, and mix in the fish sauce and sweet chilli sauce, ensuring that the rice is covered in liquid (top up with water if not). Bring to the boil, then reduce the heat to its very lowest.

Return the duck, skin side up, to the pan. Cover with a tight-fitting lid and cook very gently at the lowest possible heat for 1 hour until the duck is tender and the rice has absorbed all the liquid. Scatter over the spring onions and serve. A watercress salad is a perfect accompaniment.

# Harissa beef with steamed couscous and green beans

I love one-pot cooking, but sometimes I like the contrasts between ingredients and I don't want everything combined. This recipe makes this possible, despite being cooked in the same pot, leaving you with light fluffy couscous to contrast the rich beef stew. This is a great recipe for a wintry mid-week supper.

**Preparation time:**
10 minutes

**Cooking time:**
2 hours 20 minutes

**Serves 4**

1 tbsp olive oil

500g (1lb 2oz) braising steak,
   cut into chunks

2 onions, peeled and
   cut into chunks

2 carrots, peeled and
   cut into chunks

2 celery sticks, trimmed
   and cut into chunks

1 x 400g tin chopped
   tomatoes

500ml (18fl oz) beef stock

2–3 tsp harissa paste,
   to taste

1 cinnamon stick

1 tsp ground cumin

250g (9oz) green beans,
   trimmed and halved

350g (12oz) couscous

25g (1oz) butter

Finely grated zest of
   1 lemon

Sea salt and freshly
   ground black pepper

**To serve**
Green salad

Warm the olive oil in a casserole with a tight-fitting lid over a high heat. Add the meat in batches if necessary and cook for 5 minutes until evenly dark brown all over. Add the onions, carrots and celery and cook for a further 4 minutes, stirring often, until golden.

Add the tomatoes, stock, harissa paste and spices, then mix well and bring to the boil. Reduce the heat, cover and leave to simmer gently for 2 hours until the meat is tender.

Being careful not to burn your fingers, push a large piece of greaseproof paper (big enough to cover the meat and come up the sides of the pan) onto the surface of the stew. Scatter over the green beans and pour the couscous evenly over the top. Drizzle over 250ml (9fl oz) boiling water. Cover with the lid and cook for 10–15 minutes or until the couscous is tender.

Using a fork, stir the butter and lemon zest through the couscous and season to taste with salt and pepper. Spoon the couscous and the beans onto warmed plates and discard the greaseproof paper. Remove the cinnamon stick from the beef. Spoon the meat onto the plates with the couscous and serve with a green salad.

# Lamb and aubergine braise

This rich, dark, slow-cooked braise brings out the very best in lamb shoulder and it is also really easy to make.

**Preparation time:**
10 minutes
**Cooking time:**
55 minutes,
   plus standing

**Serves 4**

1 tbsp olive oil
850g (1lb 14oz) lamb
   shoulder, cut into
   chunks
2 garlic cloves, peeled
   and crushed
½ tsp cumin seeds
1 tsp ground coriander
2 red onions, peeled and
   cut into chunks
1 large aubergine, trimmed
   and cut into chunks
3 bay leaves, broken
500ml (18fl oz) beef stock
2 tbsp tomato purée
50g (2oz) raisins
Chopped fresh mint
Sea salt and freshly
   ground black pepper
Pomegranate seeds
   (optional)

**To serve**
Natural yoghurt
Flatbread or pitta

Warm the olive oil in a casserole dish over a high heat. Add the lamb, in batches if necessary, and cook for 5–10 minutes until dark brown all over.

Add the garlic, cumin, coriander, onions and aubergine and cook for a further 5 minutes, stirring often, until soft.

Mix in the bay leaves, stock and tomato purée, then reduce the heat and leave to simmer for 45 minutes, stirring occasionally, until thickened. Remove from the heat, add the raisins and leave to stand for 5 minutes. Remove the bay leaves.

Mix in the mint and season to taste with salt and pepper. For a special touch scatter over some pomegranate seeds. Serve with spoonfuls of yoghurt and plenty of bread to mop up the juices.

# Lamb and vegetable biryani

This recipe is perfect for all the family, and is what one-pot cooking is all about — chuck it all in, leave it to cook and take it to the table to serve, and all in **40 minutes. Perfect!**

**Preparation time:**
10 minutes

**Cooking time:**
30 minutes

## Serves 4

1 tbsp vegetable oil
600g (1lb 5oz) lean lamb
　leg, cut into chunks
1 large onion, peeled and
　chopped
3 tbsp medium curry paste
300g (11oz) basmati rice
1 x 400g tin chopped
　tomatoes
600ml (1 pint) hot
　vegetable stock
1 large sweet potato,
　about 400g (14oz),
　peeled and cut into
　1cm (½in) pieces
1 small cauliflower, about
　350g (12oz), cut into
　small florets
100g (4oz) green beans,
　trimmed and halved
Sea salt and freshly
　ground black pepper

**To serve**
Natural yoghurt

Warm a large casserole over a high heat. Add the vegetable oil and when hot, add the lamb and cook for 3–5 minutes until well browned.

Reduce the heat to medium. Add the onion and cook for a further 3–5 minutes until golden. Stir in the curry paste and cook for a minute, before adding the rice. Mix well until the grains are well coated in the paste.

Add the chopped tomatoes, stock and vegetables. Reduce the heat to low, cover and leave to simmer for 20 minutes, stirring occasionally, until just tender and thickened. Season to taste with salt and pepper. Serve immediately with spoonfuls of yoghurt.

# Lamb and sweet potato curry

This tasty curry is an ideal one-pot recipe, as it doesn't need rice — simply serve with warm Indian breads. If the list of spices puts you off, you can use 2 tablespoons of mild curry powder instead.

**Preparation time:**
5 minutes

**Cooking time:**
1 hour 15 minutes

**Serves 4**

1 tbsp vegetable oil
600g (1lb 5oz) lamb
  boneless leg or shoulder,
  cut into chunks
1 onion, peeled and cut
  into chunks
3 garlic cloves, peeled
  and chopped
2 tsp ground coriander
2 tsp ground cumin
½ tsp cardamom seeds
½ tsp dried chilli flakes
¼ tsp turmeric
400ml (14fl oz) lamb stock
1 medium sweet potato,
  about 350g (12oz), peeled
  and diced
75ml (3fl oz) natural
  yoghurt

**To serve**
Fresh coriander sprigs
Warmed Indian bread or
  poppadoms
Cucumber and mint raita

Warm the vegetable oil in a large casserole over a high heat. Add the lamb, in batches if necessary, and cook for 5–10 minutes until well browned.

Add the onion and garlic and stir-fry for about a minute. Mix in the coriander, cumin, cardamom, chilli flakes and turmeric until combined. (Alternatively, replace these with mild curry powder.)

Add the stock and bring to the boil. Reduce the heat to low and simmer gently for 30 minutes. Add the sweet potatoes and cook for a further 30 minutes until tender.

Remove the pan from the heat and stir in the yoghurt. Serve in bowls topped with plenty of fresh coriander, warmed Indian naans, chapattis or poppadoms on the side, and cucumber and mint raita to spoon over.

# Minced beef pot pie

This is perfect oven-to-table food. If you want to prepare this ahead of time, cook the mince and leave it to cool, then top with pastry and cook in an oven preheated to 180°C (350°F), Gas Mark 4 for 40 minutes or until piping hot and golden.

**Preparation time:**
15 minutes

**Cooking time:**
55 minutes

**Serves 4**

1 tbsp olive oil
1 large onion, peeled and finely diced
2 medium carrots, peeled and diced
2 celery sticks, trimmed and diced
500g (1lb 2oz) lean beef mince
2 tbsp plain flour
2 tbsp concentrated tomato purée
500ml (18fl oz) beef stock
1 tbsp Worcestershire sauce
Sea salt and freshly ground black pepper
1 sheet of ready-rolled puff pastry
Plain flour, for dusting
1 egg, lightly beaten

Warm the olive oil in a flameproof 20cm (8in) casserole over a high heat. Add the onion, carrots and celery and cook for 5 minutes, stirring often, until softened.

Add the mince and cook for a further 5 minutes until coloured. Sprinkle over the flour and stir well to combine. Stir in the tomato purée, stock and Worcestershire sauce. Bring to a simmer and cook for 30 minutes or until thickened. Season to taste with salt and pepper.

Preheat the oven to 200°C (400°F), Gas Mark 6.

Meanwhile, place the pastry on a floured surface and cut out a circle just bigger than the casserole – I use the lid of the casserole as a template. Place the pastry circle in the fridge until the meat is cooked.

Working quickly and carefully, top the casserole with the pastry. Brush the top with beaten egg and cook in the hot oven for 15 minutes or until risen and golden. Take to the table and serve immediately.

# Molten cauliflower cheese soup (v.)

Cauliflower cheese is one of my most favourite things, especially when my Mum makes it! This recipe combines all the intense, gooey cheesiness and flavours I love so much in a rich creamy soup. I like to serve this with toast spread with sun-dried tomato paste and cut into fingers ready for dipping.

**Preparation time:**
10 minutes

**Cooking time:**
30 minutes

**Serves 6**

25g (1oz) butter
1 onion, peeled and
  finely diced
1 bay leaf, broken
1 large cauliflower, cut
  into florets
1 large potato, peeled and
  diced
800ml (29fl oz) vegetable
  stock
500ml (18fl oz) milk
1 tsp English mustard
175g (6oz) mature Cheddar
  cheese, grated
Sea salt and freshly
  ground black pepper
25g (1oz) Parmesan cheese,
  grated, for sprinkling

Melt the butter in a heavy-based pan, pot or casserole dish over a medium heat. Add the onion and cook for 5 minutes until softened but not coloured.

Stir in the bay leaf, cauliflower, potato and stock. Bring to the boil, then reduce the heat, cover and simmer for 20 minutes or until the vegetables are tender.

Remove from the heat. Throw away the bay leaf and add the milk. Using a hand-held blender, blitz the mixture in the pan until completely smooth.

Stir in the mustard and Cheddar and warm over a low heat until melted. Season to taste with salt and pepper. Ladle into warmed bowls and sprinkle over the Parmesan and plenty of freshly ground black pepper.

# Paprika pork and pepper stew with rice

This is a fabulous all-in-one supper dish. You can also make it ahead of time if you need to. Cook up to the point when you would add the rice. Cool, cover and chill for up to two days or freeze for a month. When ready to eat, simply defrost, add a splash of cold water, reheat and bring steadily to the boil. Add the rice and continue cooking as directed below.

**Preparation time:**
10 minutes

**Cooking time:**
1 hour 20 minutes

**Serves 4**

1 tbsp olive oil
500g (1lb 2oz) pork
  boneless shoulder, diced
8 shallots, peeled and
  halved
2 red peppers, deseeded
  and cut into chunks
3 garlic cloves, peeled and
  chopped
2 tsp smoked paprika
1 tsp caraway seeds
400ml (14fl oz) chicken
  stock
1 x 400g tin chopped
  tomatoes
250g (9oz) easy-cook long
  grain rice, rinsed and
  drained
Sea salt and freshly
  ground black pepper
Chopped fresh flat-leaf
  parsley

**To serve**
Natural yoghurt

Warm the olive oil in a casserole over a high heat. Add the pork and cook for 5 minutes until browned all over. Add the shallots and cook for a further 5 minutes until they are also browned all over.

Stir in the peppers, garlic, paprika and caraway seeds and cook for 2–3 minutes until slightly softened, then add the stock and tomatoes. Reduce the heat to low, cover and simmer for 45 minutes, or until tender.

Stir in the rice. Re-cover and cook for a further 12–15 minutes or until the rice is tender.

Season to taste with salt and pepper and sprinkle over the parsley. Serve with spoonfuls of yoghurt.

# Quick sausage, bean and tomato hot pot

**This is a brilliant recipe that always seems to keep everyone happy in our house — my friends' kids love it, my husband loves it and I love it because it's so quick and easy to make and tastes great!**

**Preparation time:**
10 minutes

**Cooking time:**
40 minutes

**Serves 4**

8 pork sausages
1 tbsp olive oil
1 onion, peeled and
  chopped
2 garlic cloves, peeled
  and chopped
1 green pepper,
  deseeded and chopped
1 x 400g tin chopped
  tomatoes
1 x 400g tin cannellini
  beans, rinsed and
  drained
150ml (5fl oz) red wine
  (optional), or cold water
Sea salt and freshly
  ground black pepper
3 tbsp chopped fresh flat
  leaf parsley

**To serve**
Crusty bread

Twist each sausage in half, and cut, to make several smaller sausages. Warm the olive oil in a large casserole over a high heat. Add the mini-sausages and cook for 5–10 minutes until brown all over.

Reduce the heat to medium, add the onion, garlic and pepper and cook for a further 10 minutes, stirring often, until softened.

Stir in the tomatoes, beans, and wine (if using, or the same amount of cold water), and leave to simmer for 20 minutes or until thickened slightly.

Season to taste with salt and pepper and stir in the parsley. Spoon into bowls and serve with crusty bread.

# Pot-roast pork in ale with mushrooms and bacon

**I love this intense, autumnal dish. Pot-roasting pork, or any meat for that matter, keeps it wonderfully moist and full of flavour.**

**Preparation time:**
10 minutes

**Cooking time:**
1 hour 35 minutes

## Serves 6

1.3kg (3lb) pork loin
   joint, skin removed
Sea salt and freshly
   ground black pepper
1 tbsp olive oil
2 tsp butter
8 rashers smoked
   streaky bacon, diced
12 baby onions or
   shallots, peeled
2 fresh rosemary sprigs
250g (9oz) mixed, small
   mushrooms, cleaned,
   and any larger ones
   halved or quartered
3 tbsp plain flour
1 x 500ml can ale
400g (14oz) baby new
   potatoes, washed

Pat the pork dry with kitchen paper and season with salt and pepper. Warm a large casserole over a high heat. Add the olive oil and butter, and when melted, stir in the bacon and onions or shallots. Cook for 5 minutes, stirring often, until golden. Add the rosemary and mushrooms and cook for a further 5 minutes or until golden.

Remove from the heat and stir in the flour until well combined, then mix in the ale and potatoes.

Place the pork on top of the ingredients in the pan, fat-side up. Return to the heat and bring to the boil. Reduce the heat to low, cover and simmer for 1½ hours until the meat is tender and there is no pink meat remaining.

Remove the meat from the pan, place on a board and cover with foil. Increase the heat under the pan and bring to the boil. Boil vigorously for 5 minutes until slightly reduced. Cut the meat into thick slices and serve with the sauce and vegetables spooned over.

# Spicy chilli beef soup

This soup is definitely a light meal in a bowl as opposed to a starter. It's full of flavour and a fast and efficient way of feeding six people with very economical ingredients. I often make this with just 500ml (18fl oz) stock, and serve it as a quick chilli with rice.

**Preparation time:**
5 minutes

**Cooking time:**
30 minutes

## Serves 6

1 tbsp olive oil
1 large red onion,
  peeled and finely diced
500g (1lb 2oz) lean beef
  mince
2 garlic cloves, peeled
  and finely chopped
½–1 tsp dried chilli flakes
1 tsp ground cumin
2 tsp ground coriander
Finely grated zest of
  1 orange
1 x 400g tin chopped
  tomatoes
2 tbsp tomato purée
1 x 400g tin red kidney
  beans, rinsed and
  drained
1.5 litres (2½ pints)
  beef stock
4 tbsp chopped fresh
  coriander
Sea salt and freshly
  ground black pepper

**To serve**
Warmed flour tortillas
Soured cream

Warm the olive oil in a large, heavy-based pan or casserole dish over a high heat. Add the onion and fry for 5 minutes until soft and golden. Add the mince and cook for 4 minutes until sealed, breaking up any large lumps with a wooden spoon.

Stir in the garlic, chilli flakes, cumin, coriander and orange zest and cook for 1 minute until fragrant.

Add the tomatoes, tomato purée, beans and stock. Bring to the boil then reduce the heat and simmer for 20 minutes until slightly reduced.

Stir in the coriander and season to taste with salt and pepper. Ladle into warmed bowls and serve with warmed flour tortillas and spoonfuls of soured cream.

# Spicy tomato and lentil soup  (v.)

This soup is so warming and comforting! It's also a really good base for a simple dhal recipe — just add less stock (about 750ml/1¼ pints in total) and simmer until tender and thick. It also freezes really well as a soup or as dhal.

**Preparation time:**
5 minutes

**Cooking time:**
35 minutes

**Serves 6**

2 tbsp vegetable oil
1 large onion, peeled
  and diced
1 garlic clove, peeled
  and chopped
1–2 tbsp medium curry
  paste
2 x 400g tins chopped
  tomatoes
250g (9oz) red lentils,
  rinsed
1.5 litres (2½ pints)
  vegetable stock
Fresh coriander,
  to garnish

**To serve**
Natural yoghurt
Warmed Indian bread

Warm the vegetable oil in a large, heavy-based pan or casserole dish over a high heat. Add the onion and cook for 5 minutes until golden.

Add the garlic and curry paste and cook for 1–2 minutes until the onion is coated.

Add the tomatoes, lentils and stock. Stir well and bring to the boil. Reduce the heat, cover and simmer for 25 minutes, stirring occasionally, until the lentils are tender.

Ladle into bowls and garnish with plenty of coriander. Serve with spoonfuls of yoghurt and warmed Indian bread.

# Thai coconut beef curry

I'm a real fan of Thai food and this curry is no exception.
It's simple to make and has tons of rich, coconut flavour.
This recipe is based on a Massaman-style curry, but uses
standard red Thai paste, so all the ingredients are very
easy to find in your local supermarket.

**Preparation time:**
10 minutes
**Cooking time:**
2 hours

**Serves 6**

1 tbsp vegetable oil
900g (2lb) braising steak,
   cut into chunks
1 large onion, peeled
   and cut into chunks
2 tbsp Thai red curry paste
½ x 400ml tin coconut
   milk, plus extra to serve
500ml (18fl oz) beef stock
350g (12oz) potato
100g (4oz) baby spinach
   leaves
75g (3oz) natural roasted
   peanuts, roughly
   chopped
1–2 tbsp fish sauce,
   to taste

**To serve**
Cooked basmati rice

Warm the vegetable oil in a large shallow casserole
dish over a high heat. Add the beef, in batches if
necessary, and cook for 5 minutes, until well
browned.

Add the onion and stir well. Cook for 3–4 minutes
or until starting to soften and colour. Stir in the
curry paste and cook for 1 minute.

Pour in the coconut milk and stock. Bring to the
boil then reduce the heat to low. Cover and simmer
gently for 1 hour 15 minutes, stirring a couple of
times during cooking.

Peel the potato and cut into chunks. Add to the
pan and simmer gently, uncovered, for a further
45 minutes until tender.

Stir in the spinach and half of the peanuts then
season with fish sauce to taste. Ladle into bowls and
top with a swirl of coconut milk and the remaining
peanuts. Serve with cooked basmati rice.

# Summer vegetable soup with lemon and mint  (v.)

**I love this light, zingy soup in the summer — or the winter for that matter!**

**Preparation time:**
10 minutes
**Cooking time:**
15 minutes
**Serves 4**

1 tsp butter
1 large onion, peeled
  and finely diced
3 medium courgettes,
  about 380g (13½oz) total
300g (11oz) frozen petits
  pois
1.5 litres (2½ pints) hot
  vegetable stock
10g (⅓oz) fresh mint,
  leaves only
6 tbsp double cream
Sea salt and freshly
  ground black pepper
Finely grated zest of
  1 unwaxed lemon

Warm a large pan over a medium-low heat. Add the butter and the onion and fry gently for 7–8 minutes or until softened but not coloured.

Coarsely grate the courgettes and place 4 heaped tablespoons into a bowl together with 2 tablespoons of petits pois and set aside.

Tip the remaining courgettes and peas into the pan and mix well to coat in the butter. Add the stock and increase the heat. Bring to the boil and cook for 5 minutes or until the peas are just tender. Remove from the heat.

Finely shred the mint leaves (you should have about 3 tablespoons). Mix 2 teaspoons of the mint into the bowl with the uncooked vegetables and add the remainder to the pan together with the cream.

Blitz the ingredients in the pan with a hand-held blender (or use a food processor) until completely smooth. Season to taste with salt and pepper, then put back on the heat and cook until the soup is hot.

Ladle the soup into shallow bowls. Mix the lemon zest into the reserved bowl of uncooked vegetables, then spoon this mixture into the centre of each bowl and serve with plenty of freshly ground black pepper.

# Thai chicken noodle soup

Wonderfully light and delicately scented, this aromatic soup tastes really rather sophisticated! As they are not always available everywhere, I buy fresh chillies, lemongrass, ginger and lime leaves when I see them, and then keep them in separate bags in the freezer for up to three months, so I always have them when I need them.

**Preparation time:**
5 minutes

**Cooking time:**
10 minutes

## Serves 6

1 fat stalk of lemongrass, outer layers removed

1 large red chilli, deseeded and finely chopped

2.5cm (1in) piece fresh root ginger, peeled and finely chopped

1.5 litres (2½ pints) good-quality chicken stock

1 x 400g tin coconut milk

1 large chicken breast, cut into thin strips

75g (3oz) fine dried egg noodles

1 large pak choi, shredded

4 kaffir lime leaves, very finely shredded

1 tbsp fish sauce, plus extra to taste

1 tbsp lime juice

Bruise the lemongrass stalk with a rolling pin then place in a large, heavy-based pan or casserole dish with the chilli, ginger and stock. Bring to the boil over a high heat, then reduce the heat to low and simmer for 5 minutes. Remove the lemongrass stalk.

Add the coconut milk and chicken strips, bring back to a simmer and cook for 1 minute. Crush the noodles over the pan in your hands and stir in together with the pak choi and lime leaves. Simmer very gently for 3–4 minutes until the chicken is cooked and the noodles are tender.

Stir in the fish sauce and lime juice to taste then ladle into bowls and serve immediately.

# Sticky toffee apple sponge  (v.)

**What's not to like about something with sticky, toffee apple and sponge in the title?**

**Preparation time:**
10 minutes

**Cooking time:**
1½ hours

**Serves 6**

125g (4½oz) butter,
softened, plus extra
for greasing
50g (2oz) maple syrup
100g (4oz) golden syrup
100g (4oz) caster sugar
25g (1oz) soft light brown
  sugar
125g (4½oz) self-raising
  flour
1 tsp ground cinnamon
½ tsp baking powder
2 medium eggs, beaten
1 tbsp milk
2 eating apples

**To serve**
Ice cream or custard

Butter a 1.5 litre (2½ pint) pudding basin and spoon the maple and golden syrups into the basin. Place the butter, sugars, flour, cinnamon, baking powder, eggs and milk into a food processor and blitz until smooth.

Peel, core and dice the apples. Fold the apple into the sponge mixture then spoon the whole lot into the prepared pudding basin. Cover the bowl with a square of lightly buttered parchment, about 30 x 30cm (12 x 12in) and then a layer of foil. Tie tightly around the rim with kitchen string.

Place a heatproof saucer or trivet upside down into a large, heavy-based pan. Stand the pudding on top. Carefully pour enough boiling water around the pudding to come halfway up the sides. Cover the pan with a tight-fitting lid and simmer for 1½ hours until springy to the touch.

Carefully remove the basin from the pan. Unwrap then loosen the edges of the sponge with a knife. Carefully invert onto a plate — the syrup will be very hot so wear oven gloves and be careful. Cut into wedges and serve with ice cream or custard.

# Sweet cinnamon and caramel rice (v.)

My grandmother Doris made the best rice pudding in the world, baked in the oven for what felt like eons! This is my quick one-pot, stovetop version for when I can't wait that long. Suffice to say that you could bake this in the oven if you prefer — put all the ingredients into a buttered ovenproof dish and cook in an oven preheated to 140°C (275°F), Gas Mark 1 for 2–2½ hours, stirring every 30 minutes until creamy.

**Preparation time:**
2 minutes

**Cooking time:**
35 minutes,
   plus standing

**Serves 4**

2 tsp butter
200g (7oz) short-grain
   pudding rice
650–750ml (1¼ pints)
   whole milk
½ tsp ground cinnamon
4 tbsp soft light brown
   sugar, to taste

Warm a heavy-based pan over a medium heat. Add the butter and melt. Stir in the rice and mix until the grains are well coated.

Stir in the milk and cinnamon and bring to just below boiling point, but don't actually allow to bubble.

Reduce the heat to low and cook without boiling, stirring often, for 30–35 minutes until the rice is soft and creamy. Add a little more milk to reach your preferred consistency, if you wish.

Stir in 3½ tablespoons of the sugar, or more to taste. Spoon into 4 small serving dishes and sprinkle the remaining sugar over the top. Leave to stand for 2 minutes or until the sugar turns to liquid caramel. Serve warm.

# Hot chocolate pudding (v.)

This wonderfully rich dessert tastes great with its accompanying sauce, and has the most wonderful affinity with the Banoffee-ripple ice cream, from the Banoffee-bocker glory recipe on page 98 – go on try it!

**Preparation time:**
10 minutes

**Cooking time:**
1 hour 35 minutes

**Serves 6**

175g (6oz) butter, softened, plus extra for greasing
175g (6oz) light brown soft sugar
150g (5oz) self-raising flour
25g (1oz) cocoa powder
1 tsp baking powder
4 medium eggs, beaten
1 tsp instant coffee granules
1–2 tbsp milk
50g (2oz) plain dark chocolate, roughly chopped

**For the sauce**
175ml (6fl oz) double cream
150g (5oz) plain dark chocolate, broken into squares

Butter a 1.5 litre (2½ pint) pudding basin and line the base with a generous square of non-stick baking parchment. Place the butter, sugar, flour, cocoa, baking powder, eggs, coffee and milk into a food processor and blitz until smooth. Fold in the chocolate pieces.

Spoon the mixture into the prepared basin and level the surface. Cover with a square of lightly buttered parchment, about 23 x 23cm (9 x 9in) and then a layer of foil. Tie tightly around the rim with kitchen string.

Place a heatproof saucer or trivet upside down into a large pan. Stand the pudding on top. Carefully pour enough boiling water around the pudding to come halfway up the sides. Cover the pan with a tight-fitting lid and simmer gently for 1½ hours until springy to the touch.

Remove the pudding from the pan and set aside. Drain any water away and remove the trivet. To make the sauce, add the cream to the pan and warm over a medium heat until just boiling. Remove from the heat and add the chocolate. Mix well until melted. Carefully unwrap the pudding, then loosen the edges of the sponge with a knife. Invert onto a plate and spoon over the hot chocolate sauce to serve.

# In a Pan

# Balsamic-glazed steak and chips with wilted spinach

**In my opinion there's little better than simple steak and chips, and this quick solution is no exception. Vary the recipe with sirloin, rump, rib eye, or whatever quick-cook cut you prefer. Adjust the cooking time accordingly — about 3 minutes each side for medium**

**Preparation time:**
5 minutes

**Cooking time:**
25 minutes

### Serves 2

1 large potato (about 300g/11oz), unpeeled
3 tbsp olive oil
2 x 150g (5oz) fillet steaks (2–3cm/¾–1¼in thick)
A large pinch of cracked black pepper
Sea salt
3 tbsp balsamic vinegar
100g (4oz) baby spinach, washed

**To serve**
Mustard or béarnaise sauce

Cut the potato into 0.5–1cm (¼–½in) slices on a board. Warm a non-stick frying pan over a medium heat. Add 2½ tablespoons of the olive oil and the potatoes and stir to coat evenly in the oil. Fry, stirring very occasionally, for 15–20 minutes or until golden and tender.

Meanwhile, prepare the steaks on the chopping board by rubbing them with the remaining oil and black pepper. Season with a little salt.

Remove the chips with a slotted spoon and drain on a piece of kitchen paper. Increase the heat to high. Add the steak, any oil left on the board, and the balsamic vinegar to the hot pan and cook the steak for 2 minutes on each side for rare, or until browned and cooked to your liking.

Push the meat to one side and add the spinach. Stir for 30 seconds until wilted and coated in the glaze. Serve the steak and 'chips' with the spinach on the side and plenty of mustard or béarnaise sauce.

# Big brunch omelette

This generous omelette will serve a single hungry soul, or two when less hungry. It's very simple and as a result will benefit from good raw ingredients.

**Preparation time:**
5 minutes

**Cooking time:**
15 minutes

## Serves 1–2

A knob (10g/⅓oz) butter
½ tbsp olive oil
1 rasher smoked back
  bacon, diced
50g (2oz) black pudding,
  diced
75g (3oz) mixed, small
  mushrooms, such as
  chestnut or button,
  halved
Sea salt and freshly
  ground black pepper
1 tbsp finely chopped
  fresh flat-leaf parsley
3 eggs

**To serve**
Crusty bread or toast

Warm a non-stick frying pan, about 20cm/8in, over a high heat. Add half the butter and the olive oil then add the bacon, black pudding and mushrooms and stir to coat in the melted butter. Season with black pepper.

Cook, stirring occasionally, for 5 minutes, until golden. Stir the parsley through the mixture and season again with salt and pepper to taste. Push the mixture into a line across the centre of the pan.

Meanwhile, whisk the eggs together with 1 tablespoon of cold water. Add the remaining butter to the pan and melt. Add the eggs and as the egg cooks, gently push the mixture from the outside into the centre, so that the raw egg can seep down into the base of the pan.

Cook for 2–3 minutes or until just golden on the base and the egg is still wet on the top. Fold each side, right and left, into the centre, to enclose the 'filling' then slide onto a plate and serve with plenty of crusty bread or toast.

# Caramelised onion, thyme and Parmesan frittata

**This simple frittata is full of flavour and perfect for picnics, lunch boxes and even for more formal events too.**

**Preparation time:**
10 minutes
**Cooking time:**
25 minutes,
plus resting

**Serves 4**

1 tbsp olive oil
25g (1oz) butter
3 onions, peeled and
thinly sliced
Leaves from 2 sprigs of
fresh thyme
Sea salt and freshly
ground black pepper
8 eggs, beaten
60g (2½ oz) finely grated
Parmesan cheese

**To serve**
Warm crusty bread
Dressed salad

Warm a 23cm (9in) non-stick frying pan with a heatproof handle over a low heat. Add the olive oil and butter, and when melted, add the onions and thyme leaves. Season generously. Cook for 12–15 minutes, stirring occasionally, until golden and soft.

Preheat the grill to high. Pour the eggs into the pan and using a fork stir in the Parmesan and some seasoning. Use the fork to lift up the mixture, allowing the raw egg to run down into the base. Cook for 5 minutes until the base is golden.

Place under the grill and cook for 2–3 minutes until golden and just firm. Leave to rest for 5 minutes then turn onto a serving plate and cut into wedges to serve. Great with warm crusty bread and a dressed salad.

# Cauliflower, green bean and chickpea korma (v.)

**Cauliflower has a great affinity with curry flavours, so here it is combined with some other vegetables and chickpeas to make a quick and easy vegetarian dish.**

**Preparation time:**
5 minutes
**Cooking time:**
25 minutes

**Serves 4**

1 tbsp vegetable oil
1 onion, peeled and sliced
3 tbsp mild korma curry
  paste
1 small cauliflower, cut
  into florets
150g (5oz) green beans,
  trimmed and halved
100ml (4fl oz) single cream
1 x 400g tin chickpeas,
  rinsed and drained
3 tbsp roughly chopped
  fresh coriander
Sea salt and freshly
  ground black pepper

**To serve**
Warmed Indian breads

Warm the vegetable oil in a heavy-based saucepan over a medium-high heat. Add the onion and cook for 5 minutes until soft and golden. Stir in the curry paste and cook for a further minute, stirring constantly.

Stir in the cauliflower and beans to coat in the paste. Add 200ml (7fl oz) cold water, then stir in the cream. Cover, reduce the heat and simmer for 12–15 minutes or until the vegetables are tender.

Stir in the chickpeas and cook for a further 2 minutes or until hot throughout. Stir in half of the coriander and season to taste.

Spoon into bowls and scatter with the remaining coriander. Serve with warmed Indian breads on the side.

# Chicken, mint and pistachio pilaf

This might sound like a posh, complicated dish, but it couldn't be easier. The mint and pistachio give the recipe a luxurious, eastern flavour, and a great texture too.

**Preparation time:**
10 minutes

**Cooking time:**
20 minutes

## Serves 4

50g (2oz) butter
1 large onion, peeled and
thinly sliced
500g (1lb 2oz) chicken
thigh fillets, bone and
skin removed and cut
into bite-sized pieces
250g (9oz) basmati rice,
rinsed and drained
500ml (18fl oz) hot chicken
or vegetable stock
2 bay leaves, broken
1 cinnamon stick
2 tbsp finely chopped fresh
mint leaves
75g (3oz) pistachios,
shelled and roughly
chopped
Sea salt and freshly
ground black pepper

**To serve**
2 tbsp pomegranate seeds
(optional)

Melt half of the butter in a large saucepan with a tight-fitting lid. Add the onion and cook over a medium heat for 5–6 minutes until golden.

Increase the temperature, add the chicken and cook for 3–4 minutes until browned.

Add the remaining butter to the pan. When melted add the rice and stir well until the grains are well coated. Add the hot stock, bay leaves and cinnamon stick.

Bring to the boil, then cover and simmer gently without stirring for 10 minutes, or until all the liquid has been absorbed. Remove the cinnamon stick and bay leaves. Stir in the mint and pistachios and season to taste. Scatter over the pomegranate seeds (if using) and serve immediately.

# Chorizo, pine nut and pepper tortilla

I'm a big fan of chorizo, but it tastes particularly good in this dish with red peppers and potatoes to soak up its flavoursome oils. If your frying pan doesn't have a heatproof handle, invert the half-cooked tortilla onto a plate and then slide it back into the pan to cook the other side on the hob.

**Preparation time:**
10 minutes

**Cooking time:**
28 minutes,
   plus resting

**Serves 4**

25g (1oz) pine nuts
175g (6oz) chorizo,
   thinly sliced
1 large red pepper,
   deseeded and thinly
   sliced
1 onion, peeled and sliced
1 floury potato, such as
   Maris Piper, peeled and
   thinly sliced
100g (4oz) baby spinach,
   shredded
8 medium eggs, beaten

Warm a 23cm (9in) non-stick frying pan with a heatproof handle over a high heat. Add the pine nuts and dry-fry, stirring often, for 2 minutes or until golden. Remove from the pan and set aside.

Return the pan to a high heat. Add the chorizo and cook for 2–3 minutes until its orange oils are released.

Add the pepper, onion and potato and reduce the heat to medium. Turn the ingredients over to coat in the oils and cook for 10–15 minutes, turning occasionally, until soft and golden.

Add the spinach and pine nuts to the pan and continue cooking for 3–5 minutes or until the spinach has wilted. Preheat the grill to high.

Season the mixture in the pan, being aware that the chorizo is already quite salty. Pour the eggs over the ingredients and cook, lifting the mix with a fork to let the raw egg run down underneath. Cook for 5 minutes until the base is golden.

Place under the grill and cook for a further 2–3 minutes or until firm and golden on top. Leave to rest for 5 minutes, then turn onto a serving plate. Cut into wedges to serve.

# Fish and potato pan-fry with spinach, pine nut and basil butter

**This super-simple recipe looks and tastes so restaurant-y! You'll have everyone fooled whether you are serving it when entertaining or having a bit of a mid-week treat.**

**Preparation time:**
5 minutes
**Cooking time:**
25–30 minutes

## Serves 4

100g (4oz) butter
400g (14oz) baby new potatoes, halved
2 tbsp lemon juice
3 tbsp pine nuts
4 x 150g (5oz) chunky, firm white fish fillets, such as cod loin, skinned
A handful (about 10g/⅓oz) of fresh basil, leaves only
100g (4oz) baby spinach, roughly shredded

**To serve**
Lemon wedges

Melt the butter in a large frying pan over a medium heat. Add the potatoes and stir to coat in the butter. Cook for 15–20 minutes, turning them once or twice, until the potatoes are tender and the butter is nut brown in colour.

Add the lemon juice and pine nuts and cook for a further minute. Push the potatoes to one side of the pan to make room for the fish. If your pan is too small, remove the contents of the pan with a slotted spoon and set aside in a warm place.

Add the fish to the brown butter and cook for 3 minutes on each side until cooked through and opaque. Place on warmed plates.

Stir the basil and spinach through the buttery sauce (if you previously removed the potatoes to cook the fish, return them to the pan and warm over a high heat). Spoon the sauce over the fish and serve with the potatoes mixed in on the side, and lemon wedges to squeeze over.

# Emergency prawn curry

This is one of my store cupboard emergency suppers, which has saved the day on many occasions! If you don't have microwave rice, then vacuum-packed mini naan breads heated through in the toaster are great instead.

**Preparation time:**
2 minutes

**Cooking time:**
10–11 minutes

**Serves 2**

½ tbsp vegetable or
   sunflower oil
1–2 tbsp Indian medium
   curry paste, or to taste
½ x 400g tin half fat
   coconut milk
300g (11oz) frozen, raw,
   peeled tiger prawns
50g (2oz) fresh baby
   spinach, or 200g (7oz)
   frozen spinach, defrosted
1 x 280g pack microwave
   basmati rice

Warm a large frying pan over a high heat. Add the vegetable oil and curry paste and stir for 1 minute. Mix in the coconut milk and cook for 3 minutes until reduced slightly.

Add the frozen prawns and cook for 5 minutes, stirring often, until they turn pink and opaque. Add the spinach and simmer for 1–2 minutes until wilted.

Cook the rice according to the instructions on the packet. Serve immediately with the curry.

# Lamb cutlets with minty pea and potato mash

**A speedy supper dish, which tastes and looks great!**

**Preparation time:**
5 minutes

**Cooking time:**
15 minutes

**Serves 4**

8–12 lamb cutlets
½ tsp cracked black pepper
Sea salt and freshly
  ground black pepper
400g (14oz) potatoes
450g (1lb) frozen peas
25g (1oz) butter
200ml (7fl oz) vegetable
  stock
1 tbsp shredded fresh mint
  leaves

Sprinkle the lamb with the cracked black pepper and a little salt. Warm a large frying pan over a high heat. When very hot, add the lamb and sear for 2 minutes on each side.

Meanwhile, peel the potatoes and cut into small 0.5–1cm (¼–½in) pieces. Add the potatoes to the pan, followed by the peas, butter, vegetable stock and half of the mint. Bring to the boil, then cover, reduce the heat and simmer for 5 minutes. Remove the lid and simmer for a further 2 minutes until the peas and potatoes are tender, and the stock has almost all evaporated.

Place the lamb on warm serving plates. Crush the peas and potatoes with a potato masher until they are as rough or as smooth as you like. Season to taste with salt and pepper. Serve with the lamb with the remaining mint sprinkled over.

# Melting cheese, apple and walnut toasties (v.)

**Toasted cheese sandwiches are a fabulous invention in my opinion! Here I've added some apple and walnut for extra flavour and bite.**

**Preparation time:**
5 minutes
**Cooking time:**
8 minutes

**Serves 2**

25g (1oz) butter, softened
4 slices from a large walnut
   or Granary loaf
1 apple, peeled, cored
   and sliced
25g (1oz) walnut pieces
8 x 25g (1oz) slices Gruyère
   or Swiss-style cheese
Sea salt and freshly
   ground black pepper

**To serve**
Tomato and red onion
   salad

Butter each slice of bread on one side only.

Place two slices of bread, butter-side down, on a board. Divide the apple, walnuts and cheese between them and season with salt and pepper. Top with the remaining slices of bread, butter-side up.

Warm a large frying pan over a medium heat. Add the sandwiches. For best results (and I realise this isn't entirely one-pot cooking, but it tastes even better, and you'll only need to wipe the second pan) place another frying pan on top of the sandwiches to weigh them down. Cook for 2–3 minutes until golden, then turn over and repeat on the other side. Serve immediately with a tomato and red onion salad.

# Mexican chicken quesadillas

I often have chicken left over from a Sunday roast, or buy ready-roasted chicken from the supermarket. If you're like me, then why not try this easy Mexican-style toasted sandwich. It's really simple to make and tastes great too.

**Preparation time:**
5 minutes

**Cooking time:**
8–10 minutes

**Serves 2**

1 large cooked chicken
  breast, skin removed
4 flour tortillas
25g (1oz) baby spinach
  leaves, shredded
25g (1oz) grated mozzarella
  cheese (use cow's milk
  not buffalo)
25g (1oz) grated
  Cheddar cheese
2 tbsp sweet chilli sauce

**To serve**
Tomato and red onion
  salad

Tear the chicken into bite-sized pieces. Place 2 tortillas on a board and top each one with half of the chicken, spinach, cheeses and chilli sauce.

Top each one with another tortilla and press down gently.

Warm a non-stick frying pan over a high heat. Add one of the tortilla 'sandwiches' and cook for 2–3 minutes on each side, pressing down from time to time with the back of a fish slice until golden and piping hot throughout.

Remove from the pan and keep warm. Repeat with the other tortilla. Cut each one into quarters and serve with tomato salsa.

# Ten-minute tomato, rocket and Parmesan pasta

**This pasta dish is an ideal mid-week emergency meal. I always keep a jar of semi-dried tomatoes in oil in the fridge as they keep for ages, and are really versatile. If you don't have rocket, or don't usually buy it, try using shredded spinach or a handful of basil or other soft herbs instead.**

**Preparation time:**
5 minutes

**Cooking time:**
10 minutes

**Serves 2**

200g (7oz) dried pasta,
  such as penne or rigatoni
Sea salt and freshly
  ground black pepper
75g (3oz) semi-dried
  tomatoes in oil, drained,
  plus 3 tbsp of the oil
  they're stored in
50g (2oz) finely grated
  fresh Parmesan cheese
25g (1oz) rocket leaves,
  roughly torn, plus extra
  to serve (optional)

To cook the pasta, bring a large pan of salted water to the boil over a high heat. Add the pasta and cook for 10 minutes or until tender.

Drain the pasta retaining 3–4 tablespoons of the cooking water. Return the pasta and water to the warm pan. Add the tomatoes, 2 tablespoons of their oil, the Parmesan and rocket. Toss together and season to taste.

Divide between bowls and top with more rocket, if you wish. Drizzle with the remaining tomato oil and serve.

# Mussels in beer

Moules, frites and beer — perfect! When it comes to choosing the beer to use, anything goes really — beer, ale, even lager, but as with all these things, try to use the best you can or something that you would be happy to drink in it's own right.

**Preparation time:**
15 minutes

**Cooking time:**
5–10 minutes

**Serves 2**

1kg (2¼lb) live mussels
1 tbsp olive oil
2 shallots, peeled and
   finely chopped
1 garlic clove, peeled
   and crushed
1 bottle beer, about
   275–300ml
2–3 tbsp finely chopped
   fresh parsley

**To serve**
Crusty bread

Clean the mussels thoroughly under cold running water, pull away the hairy 'beards' and scrub the shells to remove any barnacles. Throw away any open or broken mussels.

Heat a large saucepan with a tight-fitting lid over a medium heat. Add the olive oil, shallots and garlic and cook, stirring constantly for 1 minute until softened.

Increase the heat to high. Add the mussels and pour in the beer. Mix well and cover with the lid.

Cook, shaking the pan every now and again, for about 3–5 minutes, or until all the mussels have opened. Remove and throw away any mussels that remain closed. Spoon into serving bowls with the juices spooned over, sprinkle with parsley and serve with crusty bread.

# Parmesan eggy bread with herby tomatoes

I love French toast, or eggy bread as we have always called it in our family. It's tasty at any time of the day, nutritious and filling. In this version, the egg-soaking mixture is flavoured with Parmesan cheese for extra flavour.

**Preparation time:**
10 minutes

**Cooking time:**
5 minutes

**Serves 4**

4 eggs
125ml (4½fl oz) milk
25g (1oz) finely grated
 fresh Parmesan cheese
Freshly ground
 black pepper
4 thick, doorstop slices
 bread (I prefer white,
 but brown works too),
 halved
4 plum tomatoes,
 at room temperature
2 tbsp finely chopped fresh
 herbs, such as chives,
 basil, parsley or mint
25g (1oz) butter

Whisk the eggs, milk and Parmesan together in a large shallow dish and season with pepper. Dunk the bread into the mixture and turn so that all the slices are evenly coated. Leave to stand for 5–10 minutes.

Meanwhile, cut the tomatoes in half and dip the cut sides into the finely chopped herbs to coat.

Warm a large non-stick frying pan over a medium heat. Add half of the butter. When hot add the bread to the pan, 2–4 pieces at a time, and cook for 1–2 minutes on each side, until golden. Remove from the pan and cover with foil to keep warm.

Repeat with the remaining slices of soaked bread, adding more butter between each batch. Two minutes before serving add the tomatoes, herb-side up, to the pan and cook for 1 minute on each side. Serve the hot bread with the herby tomatoes.

# Pesto pepper chicken and potatoes

This really easy mid-week supper tastes fantastic and works just as well with pork chops or firm fish fillets too — after searing, just adjust the cooking times up or down until cooked through.

**Preparation time:**
10 minutes

**Cooking time:**
25 minutes

**Serves 4**

1 tbsp olive oil
4 chicken breasts, skin
  removed
Sea salt and freshly
  ground black pepper
400g (14oz) baby new
  potatoes, scrubbed and
  thinly sliced
2 red peppers, deseeded
  and cut into strips
175g (6oz) cherry
  tomatoes, halved
250ml (9fl oz) dry white
  wine (or stock if you
  prefer not to use alcohol)
4 tbsp basil pesto

**To serve**
Dressed salad leaves

Warm the olive oil in a large, deep frying pan over a high heat. Season the chicken and add to the pan. Cook for 3 minutes on each side. Remove from the pan and set aside.

Return the pan to a medium heat. Add the potatoes, peppers and some seasoning. Cover and cook for 12 minutes, stirring occasionally until soft.

Add the tomatoes and the chicken to the pan. Pour over the wine. Bring to the boil, then cover, reduce the heat and simmer for 10 minutes until the chicken is cooked through.

Remove the chicken to warmed serving plates. Stir the pesto into the pepper mixture and serve alongside the chicken together with some dressed salad leaves.

# Pork chops with mustard and sticky apples

This classic combination of ingredients always works wonders, and this dish is no exception. It also works well with sausages. To complete the meal, and on days when salad won't do, I like to place my extra-large bamboo steamer filled with shredded greens or fine tender-stem broccoli, over the pan as the pork is added for the second time, ready to serve alongside. That's still basically one pot!

**Preparation time:**
5 minutes

**Cooking time:**
25 minutes

**Serves 2**

2 x 150g (5oz) pork chops
  or loin steaks
Sea salt and freshly
  ground black pepper
2 tbsp olive oil
1 eating apple, peeled,
  cored and diced
400g (14oz) potatoes
1 leek, trimmed
150ml (5fl oz) apple juice
2 tbsp wholegrain mustard

Season the pork with salt and pepper. Warm half of the olive oil in a deep frying pan over a high heat. Add the pork and apple, and cook for 5–6 minutes, turning the meat once, and stirring the apple occasionally, until evenly browned.

Meanwhile, peel the potatoes. Cut the potato and leek into 1cm (½in) cubes. Remove the pork and apple from the frying pan and set aside on a covered plate in a warm place.

Return the pan to a medium heat and add the remaining oil, potatoes and leek. Stir well and add the apple juice. Cover and cook for 10–15 minutes, stirring occasionally, until the potato is tender.

Stir the mustard into the potato mixture, then return the pork, apple and any juices to the pan. Cover and cook for 3–4 minutes or until the pork is hot throughout. Serve immediately.

# Quick pea, lemon and Parmesan pasta

I love this quick and easy pasta dish. There's something wonderfully summery about it. It's a great base too — try adding shredded cooked chicken or ham for something more substantial.

**Preparation time:**
5 minutes

**Cooking time:**
12–15 minutes

**Serves 4**

450g (1lb) dried pasta,
  such as farfalle
Sea salt and freshly
  ground black pepper
175g (6oz) frozen peas
  (I like using dainty petits
  pois for this recipe)
Finely grated zest of
  1 lemon
3 tbsp olive oil
2 tbsp chopped fresh mint
  leaves
50g (2oz) finely grated
  fresh Parmesan cheese

**To serve**
Tomato and red onion
  salad

To cook the pasta, bring a large pan of salted water to the boil over a high heat. Add the pasta and cook for 8 minutes, then add the peas and cook for a further 2–4 minutes or until the pasta is tender.

Drain the pasta and peas, retaining about 2 tablespoons of the cooking water. Return to the pan with the reserved water.

Add the lemon zest, olive oil, mint and half of the Parmesan to the pasta and toss to combine. Season to taste and serve immediately with the remaining Parmesan sprinkled over the top. Great with a tomato and red onion salad.

# Speedy pasta and meatballs

All good supermarkets sell good-quality, tasty, ready-made meatballs these days, so why not make the most of them in this quick and easy recipe.

**Preparation time:**
5 minutes

**Cooking time:**
30 minutes

## Serves 4

1 tbsp olive oil
12 fresh beef meatballs
1 onion, peeled and
  finely diced
2 celery sticks, trimmed
  and finely diced
2 garlic cloves, peeled
  and finely diced
2 large fresh rosemary
  sprigs
1 x 400g tin chopped
  tomatoes
2 tbsp tomato purée
200g (7oz) dried pasta,
  such as fusilli

**To serve**
Grated fresh Parmesan
  cheese

Warm the olive oil in a large pan over a high heat. Add the meatballs and cook for 5 minutes or until browned all over. Add the onion, celery and garlic. Reduce the heat, cover and cook for 5 minutes, stirring occasionally, until softened.

Stir in the rosemary, tomatoes and tomato purée. Bring to a simmer and cook gently, uncovered, for 5 minutes, until thickened slightly.

Pour over 1 litre (1¾ pints) boiling water and bring to the boil. Add the pasta and simmer for 10–12 minutes or until tender. Remove the rosemary.

Spoon into warmed serving bowls and sprinkle with plenty of grated fresh Parmesan to serve.

# Spicy beef fajitas

Perfect for all the family, these fajitas are lightly spiced with chipotle-smoked chilli paste. Most supermarkets sell this paste, but if you can't find it use 2 teaspoons of sweet chilli sauce mixed with a generous pinch of smoked paprika instead.

**Preparation time:**
10 minutes

**Cooking time:**
10–12 minutes

**Serves 4**

500g (1lb 2oz) lean
   rump steak
2 large peppers (mixed
   colours), deseeded
2 courgettes
2 red onions, peeled
2 tsp olive oil
2 tsp chipotle-smoked
   chilli paste
2 tsp cumin seeds

**To serve**
8–12 warmed, soft flour
   tortillas
Shredded iceberg lettuce
Guacamole
Soured cream
Salsa
Grated cheese

Cut the beef, peppers, courgettes and onions into thin strips of about the same size.

Warm a large frying pan over a high heat. When it's very hot add the olive oil and beef and stir-fry for 1–2 minutes until just browned.

Add the prepared vegetables, chilli paste and cumin and cook, stirring often, for 8–10 minutes or until well browned and sizzling.

Take to the table while still sizzling, and let everyone assemble their own fajitas with warmed flour tortillas, and a selection of fillings, such as shredded iceberg lettuce, guacamole, soured cream, salsa and grated cheese.

# Spicy sausage and fennel seed pasta

We love this tasty pasta dish at home. Adjust the chilli to taste, or serve extra alongside so everyone can add as much or as little as they like.

**Preparation time:**
5 minutes

**Cooking time:**
15–17 minutes

## Serves 2

200g (7oz) dried pasta, such
  as linguini or spaghetti
Sea salt and freshly
  ground black pepper
2 tbsp olive oil, plus
  extra to serve
4 pork sausages
1 garlic clove, peeled
  and finely chopped
¼–½ tsp dried chilli flakes
½ tsp fennel seeds
50g (2oz) rocket leaves

**To serve**
Grated fresh Parmesan
  cheese

To cook the pasta, bring a large pan of salted water to the boil over a high heat. Add the pasta and cook for 10–12 minutes or until tender. Drain.

Return the pan to a medium heat. Add the olive oil. Squeeze the sausage meat from the skins, making little pieces about the size of a large hazelnut. Add to the pan with the garlic, chilli and fennel. Fry, stirring often, for 5 minutes until lightly browned and cooked through. Reduce the heat if the garlic and spices start to become too brown.

Return the pasta to the pan. Toss together well and season to taste. Divide between bowls and top with the rocket leaves. Drizzle with olive oil and serve with plenty of grated Parmesan to sprinkle over.

# Stove-top mac and cheese (v.)

This is the ultimate convenience food without compromising on quality and taste. For a lower-fat version swap the cream for more milk if you wish — it won't be quite as yummy, but it will still taste really good. If you fancy a crispy topping on your mac and cheese, sprinkle with extra Cheddar cheese and place the pan of cooked pasta under a preheated grill until crisp and golden. Make sure the pan handle is heatproof though.

**Preparation time:**
5 minutes

**Cooking time:**
12–15 minutes

## Serves 2

200g (7oz) macaroni
Sea salt and freshly
  ground black pepper
100ml (4fl oz) single cream
100ml (4fl oz) whole milk
½ tsp English mustard
100g (4oz) grated strong
  Cheddar cheese, plus
  extra to serve

**To serve**
Dressed green salad

To cook the macaroni, bring a large pan of salted water to the boil over a high heat. Add the pasta and cook for 8–10 minutes or until just tender.

Drain, retaining about 2 tablespoons of cooking water. Return to the pan with the water. Add the cream, milk, mustard and cheese. Stir over a low heat until the cheese has melted and the sauce combines. Season to taste.

Spoon into bowls and top with more cheese and black pepper to serve. A dressed green salad is all you need to complete this meal.

# Pan-fried oranges with boozy caramel sauce (v.)

Oranges in caramel and crêpe suzette are both classic desserts. This recipe is a combination of the two, but without the crêpes! Although there's no reason why you couldn't serve some alongside.

**Preparation time:**
5 minutes
**Cooking time:**
10 minutes

**Serves 4**

3 large oranges
50g (2oz) unsalted butter
2 tbsp caster sugar
2 tbsp Cointreau,
    or other orange liqueur

**To serve**
Vanilla ice cream

Remove the zest from one of the oranges with a zester. Using a sharp knife, cut the top and bottom from the oranges. With the oranges standing on their base, cut from top to bottom to remove the skin and white pith. Cut into rounds.

Warm a frying pan over a high heat. Add the butter and leave to melt. Add the sugar and orange zest. Bring to a simmer, reduce the heat to medium and cook for 3–5 minutes until nut brown in colour.

Add the Cointreau and simmer for a further 2 minutes or until syrupy. Slide in the orange slices and any remaining juice.

Remove the pan from the heat and leave to stand for 1–2 minutes, basting the oranges in the syrup, until warm and evenly coated. Serve immediately with vanilla ice cream.

# Pears in vanilla and ginger syrup (v.)

Poached pears are such a simple dish, but always taste great. The pears are a perfect blank canvas for fragrant flavours like vanilla and ginger.

**Preparation time:**
5 minutes

**Cooking time:**
45 minutes

**Serves 4**

225g (8oz) caster sugar
1 vanilla pod
1 slice (10g/⅓oz) fresh
  root ginger (about
  0.5cm/¼in thick)
1 piece pared lemon rind
4 small pears

**To serve**
Single cream

Place 500ml (18fl oz) water and the sugar into a medium pan. Using the tip of a sharp knife, split the vanilla in half lengthways. Draw the tip of the knife along the inside of the pod to remove the seeds then place these and the pod into the pan together with the ginger and lemon rind.

Warm the mixture over a high heat until the sugar has dissolved and the water boils. Meanwhile, peel the whole pears, leaving the stalks intact. Cut a thin slice from the base of each pear so that they stand upright.

Reduce the heat to low until the liquid is barely simmering. Gently lower the pears into the liquid with a slotted spoon. Cook gently for 30 minutes, turning often to prevent them being exposed to the air for any length of time, until tender. Remove the pears and set aside on serving plates.

Bring the syrup to the boil, and continue to boil vigorously over a high heat for 10 minutes or until reduced, thick and syrupy. Discard the vanilla pod, ginger and lemon. Serve the pears with the vanilla-dotted syrup spooned over, and some cream to pour over.

# In a Wok

# Prawn and wasabi noodles

Rice noodles are such a convenient store cupboard ingredient, as they keep for ages, need very little cooking or soaking in boiling water and are a perfect foil for all sorts of Asian ingredients. They're also low in fat. Perfect!

**Preparation time:**
5 minutes

**Cooking time:**
10 minutes

**Serves 2**

160g (5½oz) dry
  medium rice noodles
2 tsp sesame oil
300g (11oz) large, raw
  tiger prawns
2 tbsp lime juice
1 tsp wasabi paste,
  plus extra to serve
25g (1oz) pickled (sushi)
  ginger, drained, plus
  extra to serve
3 spring onions, trimmed
  and finely shredded
1 tsp black sesame seeds
  (optional)

Bring 1 litre (1¾ pints) water to the boil in a large wok. Add the noodles and cook for 2 minutes. Drain thoroughly and return to the pan.

Add the sesame oil and prawns to the noodles and stir-fry over a high heat for 2–3 minutes until the prawns turn pink.

Mix the lime juice and wasabi together then pour over the noodles and add the ginger, spring onions and sesame seeds. Toss everything together well and serve immediately with extra wasabi and pickled ginger to taste.

# Chilli-beef ramen

Ramen is a style of noodle soup widely available as street food in Japan. You can buy ramen noodles in most supermarkets now, but if you have trouble finding them, just use fine, dried egg noodles instead.

**Preparation time:**
10 minutes

**Cooking time:**
20 minutes

## Serves 4

1.2 litres (2 pints)
  good-quality beef stock
3cm (1¼in) piece fresh root
  ginger, peeled and sliced
1 large red chilli, thinly
  sliced (deseed if you like
  your food less spicy)
2 tbsp lime juice
1 lemongrass stalk
500g (1lb 2oz) trimmed
  rump steak
150g (5oz) dried ramen
  noodles
100g (4oz) bean sprouts
2 spring onions, trimmed
  and finely shredded

**To serve**
Fresh coriander leaves

Warm the beef stock in a wok over a high heat. Bring to the boil then reduce the heat to medium.

Add the ginger, chilli and lime juice to the stock. Bruise the lemongrass slightly by bashing it with a rolling pin or the back of a knife and add it to the stock. Simmer gently for 10 minutes.

Meanwhile, slice the beef into long, thin strips. Add the noodles and the beef to the stock. Bring to the boil then reduce the heat and simmer gently for 2–3 minutes until the meat is opaque and the noodles tender. Divide the bean sprouts and spring onions between four bowls. Ladle over the soup and garnish with coriander to serve.

# Hoisin duck noodles

I'm a big fan of duck and hoisin as a combination — it just works so well. Here they come together in a really easy stir-fry, which is packed with flavour, colour and texture.

**Preparation time:**
5 minutes

**Cooking time:**
8–10 minutes

**Serves 4**

250g (9oz) dried, thin
  egg noodles
2 large duck breasts
2 tsp sesame oil
2cm (¾in) piece fresh
  root ginger, peeled and
  finely chopped
2 heads pak choi or Asian
  greens, shredded
4 tbsp dry sherry or
  Chinese cooking wine
6 tbsp hoisin sauce
1 tsp caster sugar
3 spring onions, trimmed
  and finely shredded

Bring 1 litre (1¾ pints) water to the boil in a wok over a high heat. Add the noodles, bring back to the boil and cook for 2 minutes. Meanwhile, remove the fat from the duck and cut the flesh into thin strips. Drain the noodles in a colander and drizzle over half of the sesame oil.

Return the empty wok to the heat. When hot, add the remaining sesame oil, shortly followed by the duck and stir-fry for 2 minutes until browned. Add the ginger and cook for a further 30 seconds until fragrant.

Stir in the pak choi, sherry, hoisin and sugar and stir-fry for a further minute until reduced slightly.

Add the drained noodles and toss with the rest of the ingredients in the pan. Cook for 1–2 minutes until the noodles are hot. Scatter over the spring onions and serve immediately.

# Easy egg-fried rice (v.)

This tasty Chinese takeaway classic is simple to make at home, and my vegetarian version is nutritious and a great way of using up leftover cooked rice and vegetables.

**Preparation time:**
10 minutes
**Cooking time:**
10 minutes

**Serves 2 as a main course**

2 tbsp vegetable oil
2 garlic cloves, peeled and crushed
2 small red onions, peeled, halved and thinly sliced
A pinch of salt
2 x 250g packs good-quality microwave rice or 500g (1lb 2oz) cooked long grain rice
75g (3oz) frozen petits pois
100g (4oz) mangetout, finely shredded lengthways
2 eggs, lightly beaten
2 tbsp light soy sauce

**To serve**
Fresh coriander

Warm a wok over a high heat. Add the vegetable oil. When hot, add the garlic, onions and salt and stir-fry for 1–2 minutes until just starting to soften.

Add the rice and petits pois and mix well to coat in the oil. Cook, stirring often, for 2 minutes.

Add the mangetout to the rice then make a well in the centre and pour in the beaten eggs. Stir and cook for 20–30 seconds until just scrambled, then combine with the rest of the ingredients in the pan.

Sprinkle with the soy sauce and scatter over the coriander before serving.

# Mexican chicken pan-fry with corn

**This easy chicken dish can be on the table from start to finish in half an hour.**

**Preparation time:**
10 minutes
**Cooking time:**
20 minutes

**Serves 4**

1 tbsp olive oil
1 red onion, diced
2 large mixed peppers, deseeded and diced
2 garlic cloves, peeled and chopped
500g (1lb 2 oz) chicken mini breast fillets
¼ tsp smoked paprika
3 tbsp sweet chilli sauce
1 courgette, diced
3 tomatoes, diced
1 x 160g tin sweet corn, drained
Sea salt and freshly ground black pepper
Fresh coriander leaves

**To serve**
Flour tortillas or nachos
Soured cream

Warm the olive oil in a large wok over a medium heat. Add the onion, peppers and garlic and cook for 10 minutes, stirring often, until softened and golden.

Increase the heat and add the chicken and smoked paprika. Cook for 8 minutes until well coloured and there is no more pink meat.

Stir in the sweet chilli sauce, courgette, tomatoes and sweet corn then reduce the heat and simmer for 2–3 minutes until softened and hot throughout.

Season with salt and pepper to taste and scatter over some fresh coriander leaves. Serve with flour tortillas or nachos, and spoonfuls of soured cream.

# Easy wok-to-table paella

**Paella is a perfect one-pot meal. Here I use chorizo and some shellfish as they are so quick to cook, but you could also use chicken, prawns or other white meats if you prefer. Just adjust the cooking times accordingly.**

**Preparation time:**
10 minutes

**Cooking time:**
20–25 minutes

**Serves 4**

200g (7oz) spicy chorizo, skinned and cut into chunks

1 large onion, peeled and diced

2 garlic cloves, peeled and finely chopped

1 red pepper, deseeded and diced

1 large pinch of saffron strands (optional)

300g (11oz) long grain rice

150ml (5fl oz) white wine

1 litre (1¾ pints) chicken stock

125g (4½oz) frozen broad beans or peas

16–20 live mussels and/or baby clams, cleaned

150g (5oz) cherry tomatoes, halved

5 tbsp finely chopped fresh flat leaf parsley

Sea salt and freshly ground black pepper

**To serve**
Crusty bread
Green salad

Warm a large wok over a medium heat. Add the chorizo and fry for 1–2 minutes until it releases its orange oils. Add the onion, garlic and red pepper and cook for 3–4 minutes, stirring often, until soft and golden.

Stir in the saffron (if using) and the rice. Stir well to combine and coat the rice in the oil. Pour in the wine and leave to bubble for 2 minutes or until it has almost all evaporated.

Stir in the stock. Bring to the boil, then reduce the heat to low and leave to simmer for 8 minutes. Add the beans or peas and cook for a further 4 minutes until just tender.

Increase the heat to high. Dot the mussels and/ or clams and tomatoes over the rice. Cover with a tight-fitting lid and cook for 2–4 minutes or until the shellfish have opened. Throw away any unopened shells. Stir in the parsley and season to taste. Serve immediately with crusty bread and green salad.

# Japanese beef and sesame noodles

This simple Japanese inspired stir-fry uses fresh noodles. Soft noodles are available at all major supermarkets either chilled or vacuum packed in the grocery section.

**Preparation time:**
10 minutes

**Cooking time:**
10 minutes

**Serves 4**

500g (1lb 2oz) trimmed
   rump steak
2 tbsp teriyaki sauce
1 tbsp groundnut oil
1 tbsp sesame seeds
2 garlic cloves, peeled
   and thinly sliced
1 large red chilli,
   thinly sliced
250g (9oz) shiitake
   mushrooms, sliced
1 x 300g pack fresh
   medium egg noodles
200g (7oz) Asian greens,
   such as pak choi,
   shredded and washed

Cut the meat into long, thin strips and coat it thoroughly with the teriyaki and half of the groundnut oil.

Warm a wok over a medium heat. Add the sesame seeds and cook for 2–3 minutes, stirring occasionally, until golden. Remove and set aside.

Return the pan to the heat and increase the temperature to high. Add the remaining groundnut oil. When hot, add the beef, garlic and chilli and stir-fry for 1–2 minutes until the meat is seared and browned.

Add the mushrooms and cook for a further minute. Add the noodles, greens and 4 tablespoons of cold water. Stir-fry for 2–3 minutes until the leaves are just wilted and the noodles piping hot. Scatter over the reserved sesame seeds and serve immediately.

# Lamb, spring green and garlic noodles with mint

I love this flavour-packed stir-fry. You can buy fresh, or 'ready to stir-fry' noodles at all major supermarkets.

**Preparation time:**
10 minutes

**Cooking time:**
5 minutes

**Serves 4**

500g (1lb 2oz) lean lamb leg, trimmed of any excess fat
250g (9oz) spring greens
20g (¾ oz) fresh mint sprigs
2 tbsp groundnut oil
3 garlic cloves, peeled and finely sliced
Sea salt and freshly ground black pepper
300g (11oz) fresh medium egg noodles

Cut the lamb into long, thin strips. Remove the core from the spring greens and shred the leaves finely – I find layering the leaves, then rolling them up like a cigar and then shredding is the easiest and fastest way to do this. Wash the leaves well and drain, but leave some water on them. Remove the leaves from the mint sprigs and throw away the stalks.

Heat a wok over a high heat. Add the groundnut oil, garlic and half of the mint leaves and stir-fry for 30 seconds until fragrant.

Add the lamb, season with salt and pepper and continue to stir-fry for 2 minutes until browned.

Add the noodles and toss with the lamb. After 1 minute, stir in the prepared greens and 75ml (3fl oz) cold water and stir-fry for 1–2 minutes or until just wilted, and the water has almost all evaporated. Scatter over the remaining mint leaves and serve immediately.

# Paneer and okra stir-fry with tomatoes and fennel seeds (v.)

**Paneer is a vegetarian, non-melting curd cheese, and okra, sometimes known as ladies fingers due to their long, tapered shape, is a green vegetable. Both make excellent accompaniments to curries and spicy dishes.**

**Preparation time:**
10 minutes
**Cooking time:**
15–20 minutes

**Serves 2 as a main course, 4 as a side**

250g (9oz) paneer
2 tbsp vegetable oil
2 tsp fennel seeds
3 garlic cloves, peeled and finely chopped
3cm (1¼in) piece fresh root ginger, peeled and finely chopped
1 large green chilli, finely diced (remove the seeds if you prefer a milder dish)
1 tsp cumin seeds
200g (7oz) okra, topped and tailed
1 tbsp ground coriander
½ tsp turmeric
1 x 400g tin chopped tomatoes
¼ tsp salt
Freshly ground black pepper
1 tbsp chopped fresh coriander

**To serve**
Natural yoghurt
Warmed Indian breads

Cut the paneer into large cubes then rub the paneer with a little of the vegetable oil and roll in the fennel seeds to coat. Warm half the vegetable oil in a wok over a high heat and stir-fry the paneer for 2–3 minutes until golden. Remove with a slotted spoon or some tongs and set aside.

Add the remaining vegetable oil to the wok. When hot, add the garlic, ginger, chilli and cumin seeds and stir-fry for 1 minute. Add the okra, coriander and turmeric and stir-fry for a further minute.

Stir in the tomatoes, 100ml (4fl oz) cold water, the salt and some pepper. Simmer for 5 minutes until thickened slightly.

Add the reserved paneer and cook for a further 2 minutes until piping hot. Stir in the fresh coriander and serve with yoghurt to spoon over, and warmed Indian breads.

# Lime-pickle prawns

**I've been cooking variations of this dish for years now and I still love it. It's so quick and simple with a great Indian flavour.**

**Preparation time:**
5 minutes

**Cooking time:**
5 minutes

## Serves 2

2 tbsp sunflower oil
250g (9oz) peeled, raw
  tiger prawns
3–4 tbsp good-quality
  mild lime pickle
1 lime
¼ tsp caster sugar
100g (4oz) spinach,
  washed and trimmed

**To serve**
Poppadoms

Warm a wok over a high heat. Add the sunflower oil and the prawns and stir-fry for 30 seconds.

Add the lime pickle, the juice of ½ lime, the sugar and spinach and stir-fry for a further minute until the leaves have wilted and the prawns are pink and opaque.

Serve immediately with the remaining lime cut into wedges to squeeze over, and poppadoms.

# Lemon chicken with almond rice

This fragrant, lemon-scented rice dish is simple to make and ready in just half an hour, so perfect for a mid-week supper dish.

**Preparation time:**
10 minutes
**Cooking time:**
20 minutes

**Serves 4**

3 tbsp almonds
2 tbsp groundnut oil
2cm (¾in) piece fresh
   root ginger, peeled
   and finely chopped
A large pinch dried
   chilli flakes
350g (12oz) mini
   chicken breast fillets
1 lemon
300g (11oz) basmati rice
650ml (22fl oz) chicken
   stock
150g (5oz) green beans,
   trimmed and halved
Sea salt and freshly
   ground black pepper

Warm a wok over a high heat. Add the almonds and dry-fry for 1–2 minutes until golden. Remove and set aside.

Return the wok to the heat. Add the groundnut oil, ginger and chilli flakes and stir-fry for 30 seconds. Add the chicken and fry for about 3–4 minutes or until golden. Using a zester, remove the lemon zest and add it to the chicken, and stir-fry for a further 30 seconds.

Add the rice to the wok and stir well to coat evenly in the oil. Pour over the chicken stock and add the green beans.

Bring to the boil, then reduce the heat to low. Cover with a tight-fitting lid and simmer for 10 minutes. Without lifting the lid, remove from the heat and leave to stand for a further 2 minutes until the rice is just tender and the chicken is cooked. Stir in the reserved almonds. Squeeze over some of the remaining lemon juice and season to taste before serving.

# Lemongrass pork in lettuce leaf cups

**This Vietnamese-inspired stir-fry is perfect for all the family. I've also made canapé versions, in smaller Little Gem leaves.**

**Preparation time:**
5 minutes

**Cooking time:**
10 minutes

**Serves 4**

500g (1lb 2oz) pork mince
1 lemongrass stalk,
   trimmed and tough
   outer leaves removed
1 large red chilli
1 red onion, peeled
3 tbsp fish sauce
2 tbsp lime juice
1½ tbsp soft light
   brown sugar
1 x 250g pack good-quality
   microwave rice or 250g
   (9oz) cooked basmati
   or long grain rice
A handful (about 10g/⅓oz)
   fresh mint leaves, finely
   shredded
16–20 Little Gem leaves

Heat a wok over a high heat. Add the mince and dry-fry for 5 minutes until browned.

Meanwhile, finely slice the lemongrass and chilli, and halve and finely slice the onion. Add them to the cooked mince and stir-fry for a further minute.

Stir in the fish sauce, lime juice and sugar and cook for 1 minute until any liquid has evaporated.

Add the rice and mix through. Cook for 1–2 minutes until piping hot. Stir the shredded mint through the pork mixture then spoon into the lettuce leaves and serve immediately.

# Quick chicken pad Thai

Travelling for three months in Southeast Asia left me addicted to the wonderful street food on offer at every corner. One of my favourites was pad Thai. It's never quite the same at home, but this speedy version is a fabulously convenient option when something hot and reminiscent of warmer climes is in order.

**Preparation time:**
15 minutes

**Cooking time:**
10 minutes

**Serves 4**

1 tbsp groundnut oil
4 tsp Thai red curry paste
2 large chicken breasts,
   skin removed and
   thinly sliced
2 eggs, beaten
300g (11oz) fresh, wide
   rice noodles
250g (9oz) bean sprouts
4 tbsp fish sauce
3 tbsp sweet chilli sauce
3 tbsp lime juice, plus extra
   lime wedges, to serve
4 spring onions,
   trimmed and shredded
10g (⅓oz) fresh coriander
50g (2oz) roasted, unsalted
   peanuts, roughly
   chopped

Warm a wok over a high heat. When hot, add the groundnut oil, curry paste and chicken and stir-fry for 2–3 minutes until golden and there is no more pink meat.

Pour in the eggs, mixing throughout, and cook for about 30 seconds until just set.

Add the noodles, bean sprouts, fish and chilli sauces, and lime juice to the wok. Toss together and cook for 2–3 minutes or until piping hot.

Scatter over the spring onions, coriander and peanuts. Serve immediately with extra lime wedges to squeeze over.

# Sticky soy chicken noodles

**This recipe is a real hit with all the family. It's quick, easy and packed with flavour and texture.**

**Preparation time:**
10 minutes, plus
  marinating
**Cooking time:**
15 minutes

**Serves 4**

500g (1lb 2oz) chicken
  thigh fillets
120ml (4½fl oz) light soy
  sauce
1 tbsp vegetable oil
2 tbsp clear honey
2 tbsp dry sherry or
  Chinese cooking wine
1 garlic clove, peeled and
  finely grated
2cm (¾in) piece fresh root
  ginger, peeled and finely
  grated
¼ tsp dried chilli flakes
½ tsp cornflour
350g (12oz) fresh, thin egg
  noodles
6 spring onions, trimmed
  and finely shredded
½ cucumber, deseeded and
  finely shredded

Remove the skin from the chicken and cut the meat into strips. Place into a cold wok with the soy sauce, vegetable oil, honey, sherry, garlic, ginger and chilli flakes. Cover and set aside at room temperature for 20 minutes.

Warm the wok and its contents over a high heat. Bring to the boil and cook for 2 minutes.

Reduce the heat to medium and cook for a further 10 minutes, turning the chicken often, until the liquid is sticky and reduced, and there is no more pink meat. Mix the cornflour with 1 teaspoon of water until smooth then stir into the chicken mixture and simmer for 1 minute.

Add the noodles to the wok and turn gently to coat in the sticky glaze. Cook for 2–3 minutes until piping hot. Scatter over the spring onions and cucumber. Serve immediately.

# Stir-fried green chicken curry

Now a regular family favourite, Thai green curry can be a bit calorific when swimming in its tasty, coconut sauce. This is my speedy, lower fat variation.

**Preparation time:**
5 minutes

**Cooking time:**
10 minutes

**Serves 2**

2 chicken breasts
1 tbsp vegetable oil
1 tbsp Thai green curry
  paste
150ml (5fl oz) coconut milk
1 tbsp fish sauce
2 tsp palm or Demerara
  sugar
3 kaffir lime leaves
  (optional)
1 x 350g pack prepared
  stir-fry vegetables
300g (11oz) fresh, egg
  noodles
1 lime, cut into 4 wedges

Remove the skin from the chicken, and slice thinly. Warm the vegetable oil in a wok over a medium heat. Add the curry paste and stir-fry for 1 minute until fragrant.

Add about a third of the coconut milk and the chicken pieces to the wok and stir-fry for 2–3 minutes until there is no more pink meat.

Stir in the remaining coconut milk, fish sauce, sugar and lime leaves (if using). Increase the heat to high, add the stir-fry vegetables and noodles and toss with the other ingredients to coat in the coconut milk. Cook for 2–3 minutes or until slightly softened. Drizzle over the juice from 2 of the lime wedges. Serve with the remaining wedges on the side to squeeze over.

# Thai beef and lime glass noodle salad

**Glass noodles are very delicate and need little cooking, so they're perfect for quick-cook recipes such as this.**

**Preparation time:**
15 minutes

**Cooking time:**
5 minutes

**Serves 4**

500g (1lb 2oz) trimmed
   rump or sirloin steak
1 tbsp groundnut oil
200g (7oz) glass noodles
   or fine vermicelli rice
   noodles
A handful (about 10g/⅓oz)
   of fresh coriander sprigs,
   finely chopped
100g (4oz) sugar snap
   peas, finely shredded
   lengthways
Juice of 1 lime
2 tbsp fish sauce
2 tsp caster sugar
1 large red chilli, thinly
   sliced (deseed if you like
   your food less spicy)

Warm a wok over a high heat. Rub the steak with half of the groundnut oil then add the steak to the hot wok and sear for 1–2 minutes on each side until browned. Remove from the wok and set aside on a board.

Bring about 1 litre of water to the boil in the now empty wok over a high heat. Add the noodles and cook for just 30–60 seconds. Remove the wok from the heat, drain the noodles under cold running water and drain again thoroughly. Return to the wok, off the heat, and toss with the remaining groundnut oil.

Slice the seared steak thinly and add the meat, any juices, coriander and sugar snaps to the noodles, together with the lime juice, fish sauce, sugar and chilli. Toss everything together well and serve.

# Rainbow stir-fry with cashews (v.)

This simple stir-fry is a great healthy, after-work meal packed with colour, crunch and flavour. If you feel you need something more substantial, add some fresh noodles and heat through thoroughly.

**Preparation time:**
15 minutes

**Cooking time:**
10 minutes

**Serves 4**

100g (4oz) cashews

1 tbsp groundnut or
  vegetable oil

1 large red onion, peeled
  and sliced

1 carrot, peeled and cut
  into thin matchsticks

150g (5oz) sugar snaps,
  halved lengthways

1 courgette, cut into
  matchsticks

1 red pepper, deseeded
  and sliced

1 yellow pepper,
  deseeded and sliced

4 tbsp sweet chilli sauce

1 tbsp soy sauce, plus
  extra for drizzling

Warm a wok over a high heat. Add the cashews and dry-fry for 1–2 minutes, stirring often, until golden. Remove from the wok and set aside.

Return the wok to the heat. Add the groundnut oil. When hot, add the prepared vegetables and stir-fry for 4–5 minutes until tender.

Add the sweet chilli sauce and soy sauce and mix well to coat all the vegetables in the sauces.

Return the cashews to the wok and mix through. Serve immediately with more soy sauce to drizzle over.

# Sweet and sticky stir-fried pineapple (v.)

This simple dessert is ready in a flash. I like to use a small pinch of dried chilli, which might sound unusual, but complements the dessert perfectly. If you don't fancy it, then feel free to leave it out.

**Preparation time:**
2 minutes

**Cooking time:**
5 minutes

## Serves 4

1 x 425g tin pineapple
  chunks in natural juice
A large knob of butter
2 tbsp soft light brown
  sugar
A small pinch of dried
  chilli flakes

**To serve**
Vanilla ice cream

Drain the pineapple thoroughly. Warm the butter in a wok over a medium heat until melted.

Add the pineapple, sugar and chilli flakes. Mix well and cook for 3–4 minutes until golden and piping hot. Serve immediately with vanilla ice cream.

# In a Bowl

# Asian chicken coleslaw

This twist on a classic coleslaw tastes great as a light meal on its own, or as an accompaniment to a summer picnic or barbecue. For a lower-fat version swap half or all of the mayonnaise with fat-free Greek yoghurt.

**Preparation time:**
20 minutes

**Serves 4**

4 tbsp sweet chilli sauce
1½ tbsp fish sauce
2 tbsp lime juice
4 tbsp mayonnaise
2 roasted chicken breasts
1 large carrot, peeled
½ x white cabbage or
  Chinese leaf, core
  removed
150g (5oz) sugar snap peas
6 spring onions, trimmed
4 tbsp finely chopped fresh
  mint and/or coriander

**To serve**
Lime wedges
Crusty bread

Mix the sweet chilli sauce, fish sauce, lime juice and mayonnaise together in a large salad bowl.

Remove the skin from the chicken. Cut or pull the meat into bite-sized pieces and add to the dressing in the bowl.

Coarsely grate the carrot and finely shred the cabbage, sugar snaps and spring onions. Add everything to the bowl together with the herbs.

Toss everything together thoroughly to coat in the dressing. Serve with lime wedges on the side to squeeze over and some crusty bread.

# Mozzarella, fennel, mint and lemon salad (v.)

Good buffalo mozzarella is *so* wonderful, and when it comes to salads and antipasti it is a must. It's a world away from the square lumps of cow's milk mozzarella, which although the better option for cooking, is no comparison to the soft, milky, clean flavour of buffalo mozzarella when eaten raw.

**Preparation time:**
10 minutes

**Serves 4**

2 fennel bulbs
20g (¾oz) fresh mint
Finely grated zest and
  juice of 1 large lemon
4 tbsp extra virgin olive oil
½ tsp caster sugar
Sea salt and freshly
  ground black pepper
300g (11oz) buffalo
  mozzarella cheese,
  drained

**To serve**
Crusty bread

Trim the fennel root and any bruised outer layers. Slice the bulbs lengthways as thinly as possible.

Remove the leaves from the mint sprigs, throw away the stalks and finely chop half of the mint leaves.

In a large salad bowl, whisk together the lemon zest, 3 tablespoons of lemon juice, the olive oil, sugar and the chopped and whole mint leaves. Add more lemon juice and seasoning to taste.

Add the fennel to the bowl and toss to coat in the dressing. Rip the mozzarella into bite-sized chunks and scatter over the fennel. Finish with some more freshly ground black pepper. Serve immediately with plenty of crusty bread.

# Herby lemon tabbouleh  (v.)

**Bulgur wheat is like a larger grained couscous, but with more bite. As it is parboiled before being packaged, bulgar only needs soaking before eating making it perfect for bowl food like this.**

**Preparation time:**
15 minutes,
  plus standing

## Serves 4

250g (9oz) bulgur wheat
4 spring onions, trimmed
½ cucumber
2 tomatoes
40g (1½oz) fresh flat-leaf
  parsley
20g (¾oz) fresh mint
3 tbsp extra virgin olive oil
Finely grated zest and
  juice of 1 lemon
½ tsp ground cumin
Sea salt and freshly
  ground black pepper

**To serve**
Warmed flatbreads or pitta

Place the bulgur into a large salad bowl. Pour over just enough boiling water to cover the wheat and cover with clingfilm or a plate. Leave to stand for at least 30 minutes or until soft and swollen.

Finely chop the spring onions. Peel the cucumber, then halve and remove the seeds with a teaspoon. Halve the tomatoes and remove the seeds. Dice both.

Remove the leaves from the herbs and chop finely (use a food processor if you'd rather). Add the prepared onion, cucumber, tomato and herbs to the bulgur wheat, together with the olive oil, finely grated lemon zest and juice, cumin and salt.

Mix everything together thoroughly and season generously to taste. Serve with warmed flatbreads or pitta.

# Mediterranean bean and feta salad (v.)

This is a great store cupboard recipe and extremely versatile. You can also add other ingredients such as antipasti vegetables if they need using.

**Preparation time:**
10 minutes

## Serves 4

5 tbsp basil pesto
Sea salt and freshly
ground black pepper
1 red pepper, deseeded
4 spring onions, trimmed
1 x 400g tin artichoke
hearts in water, drained
85g (3½oz) stoned black
olives in brine, drained
1 x 410g tin cannellini
beans in water, rinsed
and drained
100g (4oz) rocket
150g (5oz) feta cheese,
cubed

**To serve**
Crusty bread

Mix the pesto and 2 tablespoons of cold water together in a large salad bowl. Season with salt and pepper.

Dice the pepper and spring onions, cut the artichokes into wedges and halve the olives.

Add the cut vegetables and all the remaining ingredients to the bowl and toss together to coat in the dressing. Season to taste. Serve with crusty bread.

# Smoked salmon with celeriac and watercress rémoulade

Celeriac rémoulade is one of my most favourite things —
it's so simple and so tasty. I love it served with Parma ham,
but it's also remarkably good with smoked salmon.

**Preparation time:**
10 minutes

**Serves 2**

200g (7oz) celeriac
1 lemon, cut into 4 wedges
25g (1oz) watercress
2 tbsp mayonnaise
2 tsp wholegrain mustard
Sea salt and freshly ground
   black pepper
250g (9oz) smoked salmon,
   very thinly sliced

**To serve**
Crusty bread

Peel the celeriac. Slice the flesh thinly then cut the slices into matchsticks. Place into a large bowl and mix with the juice from 2 of the lemon wedges to coat.

Set aside 2 attractive sprigs of watercress and finely chop the remainder. Add to the celeriac together with the mayonnaise and mustard. Season to taste.

Divide the salmon slices between serving plates. Spoon the rémoulade into the centre of each plate and garnish with the reserved watercress. Serve with the remaining lemon wedges on the side and crusty bread.

# Japanese miso broth (v.)

This is a very easy, no-cook vegetarian miso soup. Vary it by adding extra vegetables such as shredded spring onions, Chinese cabbage and mangetout, if you wish.

**Preparation time:**
10 minutes

## Serves 1

2½ tbsp miso paste, plus
  extra to taste
½ red chilli, thinly sliced
  (deseed if you like your
  food less spicy)
1cm (½in) piece fresh root
  ginger, peeled and
  shredded
1 small pak choi, washed
  and finely shredded
75g (3oz) bean sprouts,
  washed
Soy sauce, to taste
  (optional)

**To serve**
Fresh coriander leaves

Place the miso paste, chilli and ginger into a large serving bowl. Pour over 250ml (9fl oz) freshly boiled water and stir well to combine.

Add the pak choi and bean sprouts and mix well. Leave to stand for 1 minute.

Season to taste with more miso or soy sauce.

Scatter over the coriander and eat immediately.

# Chicken and mango salad

Most supermarkets now sell very good-quality roasted chicken either pre-packed or at a rotisserie counter. They are useful for quick, convenient meals and this salad is a classic example.

**Preparation time:**
10 minutes

**Serves 4**

2 ripe mangoes
Juice of 2 limes
1 tbsp sweet chilli sauce
Sea salt and freshly
 ground black pepper
450g (1lb/about 4) cooked
 chicken breast fillets
1 cucumber
5 spring onions, trimmed
A handful (about 10g/⅓oz)
 fresh coriander, plus
 extra to garnish

**To serve**
Crusty granary bread

Cut the 'cheeks' from either side of the large, central mango stones. Peel the mangoes and cut the flesh into large chunks. Place half of the mango into a large salad bowl. Using a hand blender (or a fork or potato masher if you don't have a blender), blend or crush the mango in the bowl until smooth. Add the lime juice and the sweet chilli sauce and season to taste.

Remove the skin from the chicken. Cut or pull the meat into bite-sized pieces and place into the bowl with the mango.

Cut the cucumber in half lengthways, and use a teaspoon to scoop out the seeds and throw away. Slice thinly into slightly diagonal slices. Finely shred the spring onions and roughly chop the coriander.

Gently fold all the ingredients, including the remaining mango chunks, together to coat in the dressing. Season to taste and serve with more coriander to garnish. Great with crusty granary bread.

# Beetroot salad with goat's cheese, walnuts and sweet balsamic dressing (v.)

Beetroot, goat's cheese and walnuts is a classic combination of flavours, and comes together beautifully in this salad with a mustard and balsamic dressing.

**Preparation time:**
10 minutes

**Serves 4**

2 tbsp balsamic vinegar
2 tbsp wholegrain mustard
2 tbsp extra virgin olive oil
250g (9oz) cooked baby
  beetroot in vinegar,
  drained
A pinch of caster sugar,
  to taste
Sea salt and freshly
  ground black pepper
200g (7oz) baby salad leaves
175g (6oz) mild goat's
  cheese
50g (2oz) walnut pieces

**To serve**
Crusty bread

Place the balsamic vinegar, mustard and olive oil in a large salad bowl and mix well. Season to taste with the sugar and salt and pepper.

Cut the beetroot into wedges and add to the bowl. Mix well to coat in the dressing.

Add the salad leaves and toss to coat in the dressing.

Crumble over the goat's cheese, and scatter over the walnuts. Serve immediately with crusty bread.

# Watercress, pear and pecan salad with blue cheese dressing (v.)

This much-loved combination of flavours works so well together. As this is such a simple salad, it's worth buying the best ingredients you can.

**Preparation time:**
10 minutes

**Serves 2**

2 tsp white wine vinegar
2 tsp extra virgin olive oil,
 plus extra to serve
75g (3oz) blue cheese,
 such as Roquefort
Sea salt and freshly
 ground black pepper
100g (4oz) watercress
2 pears
50g (2oz) pecan nuts

**To serve**
Granary bread

In a large salad bowl, whisk together the vinegar, olive oil and half of the cheese to make a smooth, creamy dressing. Season to taste.

Place the watercress into the salad bowl.

Quarter the pears and remove the core. Cut into long thin slices and add to the watercress.

Scatter over the pecans and crumble over the remaining cheese. Take to the table and toss before serving. Great with granary bread.

# Beef, pink grapefruit and hazelnut salad

**This might sound like a weird and wonderful combination, but it works really well, and looks as good as it tastes.**

**Preparation time:**
15 minutes

**Serves 2**

½ tsp Dijon mustard
½ tbsp white wine vinegar
2 tbsp extra virgin olive oil
1 small shallot, thinly
  sliced
Sea salt and freshly
  ground black pepper
1 pink grapefruit
1 ripe avocado
200g (7oz) rare roast beef
100g (4oz) mixed salad
  leaves
25g (1oz) blanched roasted
  hazelnuts, roughly
  chopped

**To serve**
Crusty bread

Whisk the mustard, vinegar, olive oil and shallot together in a large salad bowl. Season to taste.

Cut the top and bottom from the grapefruit. Standing it on its base, cut with a sharp knife from top to bottom to remove the skin and white pith. Continue all the way round the fruit. Using the same knife, cut between the white membranes to release the segments and place in the bowl with any juice.

Peel and dice the avocado, discarding the stone. Cut the beef into strips. Add to the salad bowl together with the salad leaves and hazelnuts.

Gently toss everything together to combine. Season to taste. Serve immediately with plenty of crusty bread.

# French chicken and lentil salad

**Whether this is authentically French or not, I don't know, but its flavours remind me of the summer lentil salads I have often enjoyed in France.**

**Preparation time:**
10 minutes

**Serves 4 as a light meal or starter**

2 tbsp extra virgin olive oil
½ tbsp red wine vinegar
2 tsp wholegrain mustard
Sea salt and freshly ground
  black pepper
2 x 400g tins green lentils
  in water, drained
2 cooked chicken breasts,
  skin removed
25g (1oz) walnuts,
  roughly chopped
6 spring onions, trimmed
  and finely sliced
3 tbsp chopped fresh
  flat-leaf parsley

**To serve**
Crusty bread

Mix the olive oil, vinegar, mustard and some seasoning together in a large salad bowl. Add the lentils.

Pull or chop the chicken into bite-sized pieces and add to the bowl together with the remaining ingredients.

Toss everything together well and season to taste. Leave to stand for 5–10 minutes then serve with crusty bread on the side.

# No-cook chilli prawn noodles

I have been making variations of this recipe ever since returning from three months living in Asia. It's a great mix-and-match recipe, which I vary depending on what I have in the fridge! The dressing remains the consistent part, as the balance of Asian sweet, sour, salty and hot is just right.

**Preparation time:**
5 minutes, plus
  soaking

**Serves 4**

250g (9oz) fine rice noodles
4 tbsp sweet chilli sauce
2 tbsp fish sauce
2 tbsp lime juice
400g (14oz) cooked, peeled
  tiger prawns
12 cherry tomatoes, cut
  into quarters
6 spring onions, trimmed
  and finely shredded
4 tbsp finely chopped fresh
  mint and/or coriander

Place the noodles in a bowl and pour over enough boiling water to cover completely. Leave to soak for 4 minutes or according to the packet instructions. Drain the cooked noodles then cool under cold running water and drain again thoroughly. Return to the bowl.

Drizzle over the sweet chilli sauce, fish sauce and lime juice. Add the prawns.

Add the tomatoes, spring onions and herbs to the bowl.

Toss everything together to coat in the dressing. Season to taste with more fish sauce or lime juice and serve immediately.

# Hot-smoked salmon with pickled cucumber salad

Hot-smoked salmon is available in all major supermarkets. It has a great, smoky-sweet flavour, which is balanced perfectly in this recipe with the cleansing taste of the pickled cucumber. This recipe is great as a starter or light meal with buttered bread.

**Preparation time:**
10 minutes

**Serves 4**

1½ tbsp finely chopped
  fresh dill
2 tbsp white wine vinegar
1 tsp caster sugar
1 tbsp olive oil
Sea salt and freshly
  ground black pepper
1 cucumber
4 x fillets hot-smoked
  salmon

**To serve**
Lemon wedges
Buttered wholemeal bread

In a rectangular shallow dish, whisk the dill, vinegar, sugar and olive oil together. Season to taste.

Cut the cucumber in half horizontally, then in half lengthways and remove the seeds with a teaspoon.

Using a vegetable peeler, cut the cucumber into long thin ribbons. Place in the dressing and mix well to combine.

Spoon the salad onto serving plates and top with the salmon. Serve with lemon wedges to squeeze over and plenty of buttered wholemeal bread.

# Banoffee-bocker glory (v.)

**Rich toffee-ripple ice cream, flavoured with brandy, studded with banana pieces, and layered with dark chocolate biscuit crumbs and cream ... don't think of the calories, just indulge yourself!**

**Preparation time:**
15 minutes

**Freezing time:**
6 hours

**Serves 4**

300ml (11fl oz) double cream
½ x 500g tub bought vanilla custard
50g (2oz) icing sugar, sifted
2 tbsp brandy
3 large bananas
3 tbsp *dulce de leche* or good-quality toffee sauce
6 dark chocolate digestive biscuits

Place the cream into a large freezerproof bowl or tub about 2 litres (3½ pints) in capacity and whisk until thickened slightly but not quite holding its shape. Remove 4 tablespoons and set aside in a cool place. Gently fold the custard, icing sugar and brandy into the large bowl or tub of cream. Peel and finely dice one of the bananas and mix into the custard.

Freeze for about 3 hours, whisking vigorously with an electric or hand whisk every hour, until smooth. After the third hour of freezing and whisking, drizzle over the *dulce de leche*. Swirl through very lightly to barely marble the mixture – be careful not to overmix or you'll lose the ripple effect. Freeze for at least another 3 hours, or until firm.

Thirty minutes before serving transfer the ice cream from the freezer to the fridge. Meanwhile, place the biscuits into a freezer bag, seal the top and bash with a rolling pin to make coarse crumbs. Peel the remaining bananas and cut 4 attractive diagonal slices from them and set aside for decoration. Slice the remaining banana into rounds.

In 4 knickerbocker glory or tall, attractive glasses, start layering the ingredients starting with some of the biscuit crumbs, sliced banana and banoffee ripple ice cream. Repeat the process again, finishing with a flurry of the reserved cream, more crumbs and the reserved banana slices. Eat immediately!

# Mint-choc-chip ice cream (v.)

**Don't be put off at the prospect of making your own ice cream — this is such an easy recipe.**

**Preparation time:**
15 minutes
**Freezing time:**
6 hours

**Serves 4**

300ml (11fl oz) double
  cream
½ x 500g tub bought
  vanilla custard
50g (2oz) icing sugar, sifted
A few drops of peppermint
  extract
75g (3oz) dark chocolate
  chips

Place the cream into a large freezerproof bowl or tub, about 2 litres (3½ pints) in capacity, and whisk until thickened slightly but not quite holding its shape.

Gently fold the custard, icing sugar and peppermint extract into the cream.

Freeze for about 3 hours, whisking vigorously with an electric or hand whisk every hour, until smooth. After the third hour of chilling and whisking, fold in the chocolate chips. Freeze for at least another 3 hours or until firm.

Thirty minutes before serving transfer the ice cream from the freezer to the fridge. Scoop or spoon into bowls to serve.

# Rocky road

This is such a great recipe to make with children as they can mix and match the ingredients they add — try variations with dried fruit, nuts and different biscuits. I suspect that grown-ups will be equally delighted by the results!

**Preparation time:**
15 minutes

**Cooking time:**
2–4 minutes, plus cooling

## Makes 24 pieces

125g (4½oz) soft unsalted butter

300g (11oz) good-quality dark chocolate, broken into pieces

3 tbsp golden syrup

125g (4½oz) plain biscuits, such as rich tea or digestive

75g (3oz) Maltesers, chilled

75g (3oz) mini marshmallows

Place the butter, chocolate and golden syrup into an 18 x 22cm (7 x 8½in) microwaveable shallow, rectangular dish.

Microwave on medium-high for 1 minute. Remove and stir. Repeat this process until the chocolate and butter have just melted and mix well to combine. Set aside to cool for 10 minutes.

Meanwhile, place the biscuits and Maltesers into a plastic freezer bag and crush into pieces about the size of a hazelnut, the Maltesers just need to be made a bit smaller than they already are.

Fold the biscuit and Malteser pieces and marshmallows into the cooled, but not hardened, chocolate mixture. Smooth the surface and place in the fridge for at least 2 hours or for up to 12 hours. Using a sharp knife cut the rocky road into 24 fingers.

# Blackberry Bircher (v.)

I get bored of porridge, but know that oats are a good option for breakfast. This creamy muesli tastes great and is far from boring. Vary the fruit depending on the season.

**Preparation time:**
5 minutes, plus soaking

**Serves 4**

250g (9oz) oats
600ml (1 pint) skimmed
  milk
300g (11oz) 0% fat Greek
  yoghurt, plus extra to
  serve
Pinch of ground cinnamon
2–4 tbsp shelled hemp
  seeds (optional)
1 tbsp dark muscovado
  sugar (optional)
1 eating apple or pear,
  coarsely grated
250g (9oz) fresh
  blackberries, plus
  extra to serve

Mix the oats, milk, yoghurt and cinnamon together in a bowl.

Cover and leave in the fridge for a minimum of 1 hour, but preferably overnight.

When you're ready to eat, add the remaining ingredients and fold through to combine.

Serve with extra blackberries and a big dollop of yoghurt.

# Marinated peaches with Prosecco and basil (v.)

This incredibly simple dessert tastes delicious and is ready
in no time — perfect if you have surprise guests.

**Preparation time:**
5 minutes

**Serves 4**

3 ripe peaches
50g (2oz) caster sugar
10g (⅓oz) fresh basil
½ x 750ml bottle dry
   Prosecco or other dry
   sparkling wine

**To serve**
Cream

Halve the peaches and remove the stones. Cut into
slices and place into a large bowl and sprinkle the
sugar over the fruit.

Remove the basil leaves, throwing away the stalks,
and add the leaves to the peaches.

Pour over the Prosecco. Cover and place in the
fridge. Leave to steep for at least 30 minutes or for
up to 2 hours. Serve with cream to pour over.

# Coffee and walnut meringue mess (v.)

**If you like coffee desserts, then this indulgent, creamy pudding is the one for you!**

**Preparation time:**
10 minutes

**Serves 4**

2 tsp instant coffee
1 tbsp brandy
250ml (9fl oz) double cream
2 tbsp icing sugar
4 bought individual
   meringue nests
50g (2oz) walnut pieces

Place the instant coffee in a large bowl. Pour over 1 tablespoon of boiling water and stir until dissolved. Add the brandy, then add the cream and whisk until thick. Sift over the icing sugar.

Break the meringues and sprinkle with half of the walnuts over the cream. Fold together gently.

Serve immediately with the remaining walnuts scattered over the top.

# Easy raspberry mousse  (v.)

This is a bit of a cheat's mousse, but it tastes delicious and is a perfect last-minute pudding when you need one. If you're not taking the one-pot thing too seriously, spoon into individual dishes or glasses for serving.

**Preparation time:**
10 minutes

**Serves 4**

2 medium egg whites
50g (2oz) caster sugar
100ml (4fl oz) double cream
175g (6oz) fresh raspberries,
  plus extra to serve
100g (4oz) Greek yoghurt

Place the egg whites into a large bowl and whisk until soft peaks form.

Gradually add the sugar, a teaspoonful at a time, whisking well between each addition, until glossy. Fold in the double cream.

Fold the raspberries and yoghurt into the egg whites with a metal spoon, squashing the fruit and folding in as you go.

Serve immediately with extra raspberries to decorate, or cover and chill for up to 1 hour.

# Gorgeously green fruit salad (v.)

**If you are a fan of green tea then you will love this refreshing fruit salad, which tastes as good as it looks.**

**Preparation time:**
15 minutes

**Serves 4**

50g (2oz) caster sugar
2 green tea bags
2 kiwi fruit
200g (7oz) white seedless
  grapes
1 Granny Smith apple
½ honeydew or Galia
  melon
1 tbsp lemon juice
12 small mint leaves

**To serve**
Vanilla ice cream or lightly
  whipped cream

Place the sugar and tea bags in a large bowl. Pour over 200ml (7fl oz) boiling water from a kettle and stir until the sugar dissolves. Cover and leave to infuse in the fridge for 10 minutes.

Meanwhile, prepare the fruit. Peel and slice the kiwi. Halve the grapes. Quarter, core and thinly slice the apple and peel, deseed and dice the melon.

Remove the tea bags from the bowl of sugar syrup and throw away. Stir in the lemon juice.

Mix the fruit and mint leaves into the syrup and spoon into bowls to serve. Great with vanilla ice cream or lightly whipped cream.

# Strawberry and vanilla shortcakes with white pepper (v.)

White pepper is a surprising but tasty accompaniment to strawberries, bringing out their flavour. Don't throw away the vanilla pod, as it will still have plenty of flavour, so push it into packs of sugar, coffee, cocoa or hot chocolate to impart its taste.

**Preparation time:**
10 minutes

**Serves 6**

250g (9oz) ripe
strawberries, washed
and hulled
300ml (11fl oz) double
cream
1 vanilla pod
2 tsp icing sugar, plus
extra to serve
A small pinch of
ground white pepper
12 bought round
shortbread biscuits

Cut the strawberries into slices. Place the double cream into a large bowl and whisk until thickened and soft peaks form.

Using the tip of a small sharp knife, cut the vanilla pod in half lengthways and scrape the knife lightly over the inside of the pod to remove the seeds.

Add the seeds to the cream together with the icing sugar, white pepper and prepared strawberries. Fold in gently.

Place half of the biscuits on serving plates then spoon on the strawberry cream and top with the remaining biscuits. Dust with some more icing sugar and serve.

# Raspberry and limoncello cream (v.)

This simple combination tastes great and takes no time at all to make. Spoon the finished cream into little dishes or glasses and top with the raspberries before serving, if you like.

**Preparation time:**
5 minutes

**Serves 4**

250g (9oz) mascarpone
4 tbsp lemon curd
1 tbsp limoncello liqueur,
  or more to taste!
½–1 tsp icing sugar
150g (5oz) fresh raspberries

**To serve**
Biscotti

Mix the mascarpone in a bowl until smooth.

Stir in the curd and limoncello then add the icing sugar to taste.

Top with the raspberries and serve with biscotti on the side.

# In the Oven

# Bacon-wrapped pork with honey and mustard parsnips and leeks

**This recipe is great for entertaining, as it's very easy to prepare in advance and ready to cook in the oven when needed.**

**Preparation time:**
10 minutes

**Cooking time:**
35 minutes

**Serves 4**

10–12 thin rashers smoked
  streaky bacon
750g (1lb 11oz) pork fillet
3 leeks, trimmed and cut
  into chunks
2 parsnips, peeled and cut
  into short, thin wedges
1 tbsp olive oil
4 fresh sage leaves, finely
  chopped, plus extra to
  serve
2 tbsp clear honey
2 tbsp wholegrain mustard
Sea salt and freshly
  ground black pepper

Preheat the oven to 200°C (400°F), Gas Mark 6. Wrap the bacon around the pork fillet to cover it completely.

Place the leeks, parsnips, olive oil, sage, honey and mustard into a medium roasting tin. Season generously and toss everything together until evenly coated.

Sit the pork on top of the vegetables and bake in the oven for 30 minutes until the pork is cooked to your liking and the parsnips are tender.

Remove from the oven and leave to rest in the tin for 5 minutes. Cut the pork into thick slices and serve with the vegetables on the side.

# Baked lemon and olive chicken with couscous

This great all-in-one recipe is perfect whether you are cooking for family or friends. A green salad is all that is needed to accompany this summery dish.

**Preparation time:**
10 minutes

**Cooking time:**
40 minutes

## Serves 4

1 onion, peeled, halved
  and finely sliced
2 garlic cloves, peeled
  and finely sliced
4 bay leaves, broken
8 chicken thighs, skin on
1 lemon
1 tsp ground ginger
1 tsp ground cinnamon
Sea salt and freshly
  ground black pepper
2 tbsp olive oil
75g (3oz) stoned black
  olives
200g (7oz) couscous
500ml (18fl oz) chicken
  stock
A handful of fresh
  coriander leaves

**To serve**
Dressed green salad

Preheat the oven to 200°C (400°F), Gas Mark 6. Place the onion, garlic and bay leaves into the base of a large ovenproof dish (large enough to just take the chicken thighs in a single layer).

Top with the chicken, skin side up. Finely grate the lemon zest over each thigh and sprinkle evenly with the ginger, cinnamon and some seasoning. Drizzle over the lemon juice and olive oil and bake in the oven for 20 minutes until golden.

Scatter the olives over the chicken, followed by the couscous, then add the chicken stock. Cover with foil and return to the oven for 20 minutes until the couscous is tender.

Remove from the oven. Use a fork to fluff up and separate the grains of couscous. Scatter the fresh coriander leaves over the top. Take to the table and serve immediately with a dressed green salad.

# Moroccan lamb with roasted ratatouille

To make this recipe, ask your butcher to bone-out and butterfly a leg of lamb for you, or look in the supermarket for a 'lamb leg boneless joint'. Harissa paste is a chilli-hot, Moroccan-spiced paste available from all major supermarkets.

**Preparation time:**
15 minutes

**Cooking time:**
about 40 minutes

**Serves 6**

800g–1kg (1¾–2¼lb)
  boneless lamb leg joint
2–3 tsp harissa paste
3 large courgettes,
  trimmed and cut
  into chunks
3 peppers (mixed colours),
  deseeded and cut
  into chunks
1 large aubergine, cut
  into chunks
2 red onions, peeled
  and cut into wedges
500g (1lb 2oz) baby new
  potatoes
1 x 400g tin chopped
  tomatoes
3 garlic cloves, peeled
  and roughly chopped
1 tbsp olive oil
15g (½oz) fresh oregano,
  chopped
Juice of 1 lemon
Sea salt and freshly
  ground black pepper

Preheat the oven to 220°C (425°F), Gas Mark 7. Unroll the lamb and lay it skin side down. Slash any thick parts to make the meat of an even thickness all over. Rub the harissa paste all over the meat.

Place the prepared vegetables, tomatoes, garlic, olive oil, oregano and lemon juice into a large roasting tin. Season well with salt and pepper and toss all the ingredients together.

Place a rack over the vegetables and lay the lamb out flat on top, skin side up. Place into the oven and immediately reduce the temperature to 190°C (350°F), Gas Mark 4. Cook for 40 minutes, or until the lamb is browned and the vegetables are tender.

Remove from the oven and cover the whole lot in foil, with the meat still on the rack over the vegetables. Leave to rest for 5 minutes. Remove the foil and transfer the meat to a board. Carve the meat into thick slices. Mix any roasting juices into the vegetables and season to taste. Serve alongside the lamb.

# Baked garlic mushroom risotto

Risotto can be time-consuming to make, so this all-in-one baked version is perfect, as the oven does all the work for you.

**Preparation time:**
10 minutes

**Cooking time:**
60 minutes

## Serves 4

25g (1oz) butter, for
   greasing
350g (12oz) mixed
   mushrooms, cleaned
2 garlic cloves, peeled
   and finely chopped
1 tbsp fresh thyme leaves
150ml (5fl oz) white wine
Sea salt and freshly
   ground black pepper
300g (11oz) risotto rice
700ml (23fl oz) vegetable
   stock
50g (2oz) finely grated
   fresh Parmesan cheese,
   plus extra to serve

**To serve**
Dressed green salad

Preheat the oven to 180°C (350°F), Gas Mark 4. Butter an ovenproof dish generously. Cut any large mushrooms into bite-sized pieces and place into the dish with the garlic, thyme and white wine. Season generously with salt and pepper.

Roast in the oven for 20 minutes, stirring once during cooking. Add the rice and mix well to coat in the liquid. Add the vegetable stock. Cover with a tight-fitting lid or foil and return to the oven.

Place into the oven and cook without stirring for 40 minutes or until much of the liquid is absorbed and the rice is just tender.

Remove the risotto from the oven and stir in the grated Parmesan for about 1–2 minutes or until the rice is creamy. Season to taste. Serve immediately with dressed green salad.

# Roasted chicken tikka and sag aloo

**I love this recipe! It makes light work of two of my favourite Indian dishes in one! Serve with some warmed Indian breads or freshly cooked basmati rice.**

**Preparation time:**
10 minutes
**Cooking time:**
40 minutes

## Serves 4

1 small chicken, about
  1.2–1.5kg (2½–3lb 6oz)
  in weight
4 tbsp tikka curry paste
2 onions, peeled and cut
  into wedges
750g (1lb 11oz) potatoes,
  peeled and cut into
  chunks
3 garlic cloves, peeled
  and roughly chopped
1 tsp cumin seeds
1 tsp ground coriander
1 tbsp vegetable oil
Sea salt and freshly
  ground black pepper
100g (4oz) baby spinach
  leaves

**To serve**
Natural yoghurt
Warmed Indian breads or
  cooked basmati rice

Preheat the oven to 200°C (400°F), Gas Mark 6. Place the chicken breast side down and, using a pair of scissors, cut either side of the back bone and remove it. Turn the chicken back over, open it out and press down with the heel of your hand to flatten. Rub the chicken all over with the curry paste.

Place the onions, potatoes, garlic, cumin seeds, coriander and vegetable oil into a large roasting tin and mix together thoroughly. Season with a little salt and pepper.

Place a rack over the tin and sit the chicken, skin side up, on top. Place the whole lot into the oven and roast for 40 minutes or until the chicken is golden and the juices run clear when tested.

Remove the chicken and leave it to rest on a board or platter. Meanwhile, stir the spinach into the potato mixture, scraping up any sticky bits from the base of the tin, until the spinach is well combined and wilted. Season to taste. Carve the chicken. Serve the potato and spinach mixture alongside the chicken with yoghurt to spoon over.

# Lamb shanks with tomatoes and lentils

**Beautifully tender lamb with little effort, this dish is perfect both for the family or when entertaining friends.**

**Preparation time:**
5 minutes

**Cooking time:**
1 hour 50 minutes

**Serves 4**

4 lamb shanks

2 x 400g tins chopped
   tomatoes

1 red onion, peeled
   and diced

2 garlic cloves, peeled
   and roughly chopped

700ml (23fl oz) beef or
   lamb stock

250ml (9fl oz) red wine

2 tbsp soft light brown
   sugar

4 fresh rosemary sprigs

275g (10oz) green or Puy
   lentils, rinsed and
   drained

100g (4oz) baby spinach
   leaves

Sea salt and freshly
   ground black pepper

Preheat the oven to 200°C (400°F), Gas Mark 6.

Place the lamb into an ovenproof dish just large enough to take the lamb in a single layer. Pour over the tomatoes and scatter over the onion, garlic, stock, wine, sugar and rosemary. Cover with foil or a tight-fitting lid and bake in the oven for 60 minutes.

Turn the lamb over, add the lentils and stir to immerse in the liquid. Re-cover with the lid or foil and cook for a further 40 minutes or until the lamb and lentils are tender.

Remove the lid or foil and cook for a further 10 minutes until the lamb browns slightly.

Remove from the oven and stir in the spinach. Season to taste before spooning onto warmed serving plates.

# Warm Italian bread salad with tomatoes and mozzarella (v.)

My version of a classic Italian salad is extremely easy to make and packed with summer flavours. Use your tomatoes at room temperature to get the most from their flavour, as a cold, refrigerated tomato won't taste of anything!

**Preparation time:**
10 minutes

**Cooking time:**
10 minutes,
   plus cooling

**Serves 4**

150g (5oz) ciabatta bread
225g (8oz) cherry tomatoes
3 tbsp olive oil
1 garlic clove, peeled
   and finely chopped
Sea salt and freshly
   ground black pepper
20g (¾oz) fresh basil sprigs
20g (¾oz) fresh flat-leaf
   parsley sprigs
250g (9oz/about 3) plum
   tomatoes, cut into
   wedges
125g (4½oz) buffalo
   mozzarella cheese, torn
   into chunks
1 tbsp red wine vinegar

Preheat the oven to 200°C (400°F), Gas Mark 6. Rip the ciabatta into bite-sized chunks and place into a large roasting tin with the cherry tomatoes. Drizzle over 2 tablespoons of the olive oil and toss together with the garlic and some seasoning until well coated in the oil.

Bake in the oven for 10 minutes or until the bread is golden. Remove the tin from the oven and leave to cool for 5 minutes.

Meanwhile, remove the basil and parsley leaves from the stalks (throw the stalks away).

Add the raw plum tomatoes, basil and parsley leaves and mozzarella to the tin and drizzle over the vinegar and remaining olive oil. Season generously and mix gently to combine. Eat immediately while the bread is warm and crispy.

# Bacon and egg 'pies'

**Great for a light meal or brunch with buttered bread, these 'pies' taste delicious and are quick to make.**

**Preparation time:**
10 minutes

**Cooking time:**
15 minutes

**Serves 6**

Butter, for greasing
  and spreading
12 rashers thin-cut
  smoked streaky bacon
12 medium free-range eggs
3 tbsp double cream
2 tbsp chopped fresh flat
  leaf parsley
2 tbsp finely grated fresh
  Parmesan cheese
Sea salt and freshly ground
  black pepper

**To serve**
6–12 slices of thick-cut
  bread, buttered

Preheat the oven to 180°C (350°F), Gas Mark 4. Butter a 12-hole muffin tin.

Line the base and sides of each hole with a bacon rasher, wrapping each one around in a spiral.

Crack an egg into each hole. Divide the cream, parsley, Parmesan and plenty of seasoning between each one.

Place in the oven for 15 minutes until the eggs are just set. Leave to cool for 2–3 minutes then run a knife around the outside of each one to loosen. Serve hot with plenty of buttered bread. If you prefer toast simply put the bread into the oven at the same time as the eggs and cook until golden.

# Easy mushroom, tomato and Brie pies (v.)

This smart vegetarian recipe is perfect for entertaining. Vegetarian Brie is widely available, although if you struggle to find it, you can use any alternative that's gooey and melts well.

**Preparation time:**
15 minutes

**Cooking time:**
20 minutes

**Serves 4**

A little butter, for greasing
4 large portabello or
　field mushrooms, about
　8–10cm (3–4in) across
Sea salt and freshly
　ground black pepper
50g (2oz) baby spinach
　leaves
2 tbsp semi-dried
　tomatoes in oil, drained
125g (4½oz) Brie
375g (13oz) bought,
　ready-rolled puff pastry
A little milk or beaten
　egg, to glaze

**To serve**
Dressed salad leaves

Preheat the oven to 200°C (400°F), Gas Mark 6, and lightly butter a baking sheet. Brush the mushrooms clean with kitchen paper. Using a teaspoon, remove the stalks and set aside. Place the mushrooms, gill side up, on the baking sheet and season with salt and pepper.

Roughly chop the removed mushroom stalks, spinach and tomatoes. Cut the Brie into cubes. Season with salt and pepper and mix the whole lot together on the chopping board. If the mixture looks very dry add up to 1 tablespoon of the tomato oil.

Pile the spinach and Brie mixture into the mushroom shells as evenly as possible. Using a 10–12cm (4–5in) cutter, stamp out 4 rounds of pastry. Top each filled mushroom with a pastry round and brush with a little milk or egg to glaze.

Bake in the oven for 20 minutes until risen and golden. Serve immediately with some dressed salad leaves.

# Chicken and spring vegetable parcels

**Wrapping ingredients in parchment parcels and then cooking them in the oven is a great way of sealing in all the natural juices and flavours, and it also makes a great all-in-one meal, ready to be opened at the table for dramatic effect.**

**Preparation time:**
10 minutes

**Cooking time:**
20–25 minutes

**Serves 4**

300g (11oz) baby new
   potatoes, sliced thinly
150g (5oz) green beans,
   trimmed
12 asparagus spears,
   woody ends removed
4 skinless chicken breasts
Grated zest of 1 lemon
25g (1oz) butter
4 tbsp white wine
Sea salt and freshly
   ground black pepper

Preheat the oven to 200°C (400°F), Gas Mark 6. Cut 4 x 30cm (12in) squares from non-stick baking parchment.

Divide the potato slices between the paper squares then top with the beans, asparagus and a piece of chicken.

Scatter over the lemon zest, dot with butter and drizzle over the wine and season with salt and pepper. Fold the paper over the contents then fold or scrunch over the top and sides to seal tightly, tucking the ends underneath the parcel – leave enough room for steam to gather inside the parcel.

Place on a baking sheet and cook in the oven for 20–25 minutes until the vegetables are tender, the chicken is cooked through and the juices run clear when a skewer is inserted into the thickest part of the meat. Place a parcel on each serving plate and open at the table being careful of the escaping steam.

# Oven-baked chicken and tomato risotto

This is perfect family food — it's quick, easy and nutritious, especially when served with a green salad.

**Preparation time:**
10 minutes

**Cooking time:**
45 minutes

**Serves 4**

4 skinless chicken breasts, about 500g (1lb 2oz) in total
300g (11oz) risotto rice
500ml (18fl oz) chicken stock
1 x 400g tin chopped tomatoes
50g (2oz) finely grated fresh Parmesan cheese, plus extra to serve
25g (1oz) butter
Sea salt and freshly ground black pepper

**To serve**
Dressed green salad

Preheat the oven to 180°C (350°F), Gas Mark 4. Cut the chicken into chunks.

Place the rice, chicken stock, tomatoes and chicken into an ovenproof casserole dish with a tight-fitting lid. Stir well and cover.

Cook in the oven, without stirring for 45 minutes or until much of the liquid is absorbed and the rice is just tender.

Remove the risotto from the oven and stir in the Parmesan and butter for about 1–2 minutes or until the rice is creamy. Season to taste. Serve immediately with dressed green salad.

# Celeriac and Parma ham bake

Celeriac and Parma ham is a match made in heaven in my opinion, and it tastes perfect in this comforting, rich bake. If you don't have Parma ham, cooked bacon or ham will suffice, but won't be quite as good! Serve with salad or green beans with a zingy dressing to cut through the richness of the dish.

**Preparation time:**
10 minutes

**Cooking time:**
1–1 ½ hours

**Serves 6**

1 garlic clove, peeled
    and halved
A little butter, for greasing
2 x 500g (1lb 2 oz) celeriac
8 wafer thin slices Parma
    ham, about 100g (4oz)
1 tbsp fresh thyme leaves
Sea salt and freshly
    ground black pepper
500ml (18fl oz) double
    cream
300ml (11fl oz) whole milk

**To serve**
Green salad

Preheat the oven to 160°C (315°F), Gas Mark 2–3. Rub the cut side of the garlic thoroughly over the inner surface of a 2 litre (3½ pint) ovenproof dish and butter the dish.

Finely slice the remaining garlic. Peel, quarter and thinly slice the celeriac. Layer the celeriac, Parma ham, garlic and thyme leaves in several alternate layers, seasoning well between each one, until all the ingredients have been used up. End with a layer of celeriac.

Steadily pour over the cream and milk, giving it time to seep into each and every layer between each addition.

Cover with foil and cook in the oven for 45 minutes, then remove the foil and cook for a further 45 minutes until tender and golden. Remove from the oven and leave to stand for 5 minutes before serving with a green salad.

# Really quick fish pie

This cheat's pie is so quick to make and yet wonderfully comforting. I often cook this at home as the fish and sauce all freeze well so are easily defrosted during the day ready for action on my return. The breadcrumbs are, to my mind, a store cupboard ingredient — if I have some bread hanging around uneaten I'll blitz it and put the crumbs in the freezer — it really isn't a case of being a domestic goddess, I'm not. But it takes a matter of seconds and the crumbs are endlessly useful for dishes such as this speedy 'pie'.

**Preparation time:**
10 minutes

**Cooking time:**
20 minutes

## Serves 2

300g (11oz) cod loin, or
  other firm white fish
  fillets, skinned
150g (5oz) raw peeled
  tiger or king prawns
About 20 fresh chives
  (optional)
Sea salt and freshly
  ground black pepper
1 x 350g tub good-quality
  supermarket white or
  cheese sauce
A generous handful
  (about 25g/1oz) fresh
  breadcrumbs

**To serve**
Dressed tomato and red
  onion salad

Preheat the oven to 190°C (375°F), Gas Mark 5.

Place the fish into an ovenproof dish and scatter over the prawns. Snip the chives over the top with a pair of scissors and season with salt and pepper.

Pour over the sauce and scatter the breadcrumbs over the top.

Bake in the oven for 20 minutes or until bubbling and golden. Serve immediately with a dressed tomato and red onion salad.

# Roasted pepper, rocket and goat's cheese lasagne

Lasagne can be quite complicated as there are a lot of different elements to prepare before assembly, but this veggie lasagne couldn't be easier. Use jars of roasted red peppers for convenience, or chargrill your own if you wish (you'll need about 10 large, fresh red peppers).

**Preparation time:**
10 minutes

**Cooking time:**
30 minutes

**Serves 6**

1 x 500ml tub crème fraîche
100ml (4fl oz) milk
2 eggs, beaten
4 tbsp grated fresh
  Parmesan cheese
Sea salt and freshly
  ground black pepper
1 x 700g jar roasted red
  peppers, drained
200g (7oz) soft goat's cheese
50g (2oz) pine nuts, toasted
  (see page 39)
150g (5oz) rocket leaves,
  roughly chopped
8 fresh lasagne sheets

**To serve**
Crisp green salad

Preheat the oven to 190°C (375°F), Gas Mark 5. Whisk the crème fraîche, milk and eggs together with half of the Parmesan. Season generously. Open the peppers out so they are flat and dry both sides with kitchen paper.

Spoon a third of the prepared sauce mixture over the base of an 20 x 26cm (8 x 10½in) ovenproof dish. Place half of the peppers in a single layer over the top.

Crumble half of goat's cheese over the peppers, followed by a third of the pine nuts and half of the rocket. Season well then top with half of the lasagne sheets, overlapping them so that they completely cover the ingredients in the dish.

Repeat this process again, ending with the final third of sauce. Spread with the back of a spoon so that it completely covers the lasagne. Scatter the remaining Parmesan and pine nuts over the top.

Bake in the oven for 30 minutes or until golden, risen and piping hot throughout. Remove from the oven and leave to stand for 5 minutes before cutting into portions and serving with a crisp green salad.

# Roast beef with vegetables and giant Yorkshire pudding

**This family favourite is made even better by becoming a one-pot meal.**

**Preparation time:**
15 minutes
**Cooking time:**
1 hour 40 minutes

### Serves 6

1.5kg (3lb 6oz) boneless
beef roasting joint, such
as boneless fore rib
Sea salt and freshly
ground black pepper
3 large carrots
2 leeks, rinsed
1 swede, 625g (1lb 6oz)
1 celeriac, 750g (1lb 11oz)
6 garlic cloves, peeled
3 fresh thyme sprigs,
leaves only
2 tbsp olive oil

**For the Yorkshire pudding**
175g (6oz) plain flour
A large pinch of salt
3 medium eggs
225ml (8fl oz) milk
225ml (8fl oz) water

**To serve**
Horseradish sauce

Preheat the oven to 220°C (425°F), Gas Mark 7. Place the beef fat side up in a large roasting tin, about 25 x 35cm (10 x 14in) is about right. Season generously and roast in the oven for 30 minutes.

Meanwhile, prepare the vegetables, peeling where necessary, and cut them into 2cm (¾in) chunks (do the celeriac last so it doesn't have a chance to turn brown). When the beef has been cooking for 30 minutes remove from the oven and scatter the vegetables around the beef. Add the garlic, thyme and the olive oil and mix well with a spoon until thoroughly coated. Return to the oven, reduce the temperature to 180°C (350°F), Gas Mark 4 and cook for a further 70 minutes.

Meanwhile, whisk all the Yorkshire pudding ingredients together in a large bowl until smooth. Cover and leave to rest. After the beef has finished cooking, remove the tin from the oven and increase the oven temperature back up to 220°C (425°F), Gas Mark 7.

Place the beef on a board or platter. Cover with 2 layers of foil and leave to rest. Turn the vegetables in the tin over with a spoon to coat in the oil again and spread them out evenly over the base of the tin. Return to the oven for 5 minutes.

Pour the Yorkshire pudding batter over the vegetables and cook for a further 15–20 minutes or until risen and golden. Cut the pudding into large pieces and carve the meat. Serve with plenty of horseradish sauce.

# Maple-glazed sausages and butternut mash

This is such a comforting autumnal recipe packed with flavour and wonderful colour.

**Preparation time:**
10 minutes

**Cooking time:**
30–35 minutes

## Serves 2

8–12 sausages
1 large butternut squash,
  about 1.2kg (2½lb)
2 garlic cloves, peeled
  and finely sliced
1 tbsp olive oil
2 tbsp maple syrup
1 tbsp English mustard
A pinch of dried thyme
Sea salt and freshly
  ground black pepper

**To serve**
Salad leaves

Preheat the oven to 190°C (375°F), Gas Mark 5. Place the sausages into a large roasting tin. Halve and peel the squash, then remove the seeds with a spoon. Cut the squash into chunks and add to the roasting tin together with the garlic.

Add the olive oil, maple syrup, mustard and thyme and toss everything together until evenly coated. Season generously.

Roast in the oven for 30–35 minutes, turning everything once during cooking, until the sausages are brown and cooked through.

Remove the sausages from the tin and keep warm. Leaving the squash in the tin, mash it until it's as smooth or as chunky as you like it! Season to taste and serve with the sausages and some salad leaves.

# Creamy potato and blue cheese gratin (v.)

**This is a very rich but wonderfully delicious gratin. Serve with some leaves and an acidic dressing to cut through the richness.**

**Preparation time:**
15 minutes

**Cooking time:**
1 hour 30 minutes

## Serves 6

1 tbsp butter, for greasing
1kg (2¼lb) waxy potatoes,
　such as King Edward
150g (5oz) blue cheese,
　crumbled
Sea salt and freshly
　ground black pepper
600ml (1 pint) double
　cream
200ml (7fl oz) milk

**To serve**
Chicory or watercress

Preheat the oven to 160°C (315°F), Gas Mark 2–3. Butter a large ovenproof dish.

Peel the potatoes and slice very thinly, about the thickness of a £1 coin.

Layer the potatoes into the dish, intermittently adding a layer of crumbled blue cheese, and seasoning (being cautious with the salt as blue cheese is quite salty already). End with a layer of potatoes. Slowly pour over the cream and milk, bit by bit, giving it time to seep in.

Cover with foil and bake in the oven for 45 minutes. Remove the foil and cook for a further 45 minutes or until golden on the top and the potato is tender when tested with the tip of a knife. Remove from the oven and leave to rest for 5 minutes before serving with the chicory or watercress.

# Oven fish and chips

Fish and chips are such a favourite but high in fat. This oven-cooked version is light and tasty — plenty of indulgence without the side order of guilt!

**Preparation time:**
10 minutes
**Cooking time:**
35 minutes

### Serves 4

800g (1¾lb) potatoes,
  such as King Edward
2 garlic cloves, peeled
  and sliced
1 tsp dried oregano
3 tbsp olive oil
Sea salt and freshly
  ground black pepper
4 x 150g (5oz) firm white
  fish fillets, such as
  haddock or pollack
4 sprigs of cherry
  tomatoes on the vine

**To serve**
Lemon wedges or
  malt vinegar

Preheat the oven to 200°C (400°F), Gas Mark 6. Cut the potatoes into thick wedges or chips.

Place in a large roasting pan with the garlic, half of the oregano and 2 tablespoons of the olive oil. Season well and toss everything together to coat in the oil.

Bake in the oven for 30 minutes, turning them over halfway through, until tender and golden. Push the chips to one side to make room for the fish and tomatoes and add the fish and tomatoes to the pan. Drizzle with the remaining olive oil, oregano and some salt and pepper.

Bake for a further 5 minutes or until the fish is opaque and the tomatoes are soft. Discard the garlic. Divide between serving plates and serve with lemon wedges or malt vinegar to drizzle over.

# Orange and cranberry granola (v.)

**Keep this crunchy granola for up to four weeks in an airtight container. I like to vary the recipe with other nuts, seeds and dried fruit, depending on what I fancy and what's in the cupboard.**

**Preparation time:**
5 minutes

**Cooking time:**
25–35 minutes, plus
  cooling

**Serves 4—6**

250g (9oz) large rolled oats
100g (4oz) pecans,
  roughly chopped
4–6 tbsp runny honey,
  to taste
Finely grated zest of
  1 orange
25g (1oz) butter, diced
100g (4oz) dried
  cranberries

**To serve**
Fresh, chilled milk

Preheat the oven to 160°C (315°F), Gas Mark 2–3. Tip the oats and pecans into a large roasting tin and place in the oven for 5 minutes.

Drizzle over the honey, adding as much or as little as you like, depending on how sweet you like it. Scatter over the finely grated zest from the orange and the butter.

Put back in the oven for 20–30 minutes, stirring every now and again, until golden.

Remove from the oven and leave to cool if you can resist it for that long. Add the cranberries and serve with the segments from the orange and fresh chilled milk.

# Easy apple pies (v.)

**Some ingredients are great tinned, and apple, when making pies, crumbles and the like, is one of them.**

**Preparation time:**
10 minutes

**Cooking time:**
15–20 minutes

**Serves 4**

375g (13oz) sheet
    ready-rolled puff pastry
Plain flour, for dusting
1 x 200g tin sliced apple,
    drained
3 tsp caster sugar
1 egg, lightly beaten
2 tsp demerara sugar

**To serve**
Cream, ice cream
    or custard

Preheat the oven to 200°C (400°F), Gas Mark 6. Place the pastry on a floured surface. Using an 8cm (3in) cutter (I usually cut round an espresso saucer if I'm in a rush), stamp out 4 rounds. Do the same with a 10cm (4in) cutter to make another 4 slightly larger rounds, re-rolling the pastry if necessary.

Place the 4 smaller pastry rounds on a non-stick baking sheet. Divide the apple between them, leaving a border of pastry around the edge and sprinkle over the caster sugar. Brush a little egg onto the pastry borders and top with the remaining large pastry discs. Pinch the edges of the pastry together neatly to seal.

Brush with egg, sprinkle over the demerara sugar and use the tip of a sharp knife to make a slit in the top of each one.

Bake in the oven for 20 minutes or until golden and risen. Remove from the oven and leave to cool slightly before serving with plenty of cream, ice cream or custard.

# Sticky ginger bread and butter pudding (v.)

Bread and butter pudding is one of my favourite puddings. It's also incredibly versatile. If, like me, you hate peel and dried fruit, just leave it out as I have here. Or spread the buttered bread with marmalade, or even chocolate spread, to customise it. For me, sticky stem ginger is a fabulous addition, so here it is.

**Preparation time:**
15 minutes,
plus soaking

**Cooking time:**
30–35 minutes

**Serves 6**

50g (2oz) butter, softened
8 slices white bread,
crusts removed
3 eggs
500ml (18fl oz) milk
50g (2oz) caster sugar
1 tsp vanilla extract
2 pieces of stem ginger,
plus 3 tbsp of the syrup
it's stored in

**To serve**
Cream

Preheat the oven to 180°C (350°F), Gas Mark 4. Butter the bread, remove the crusts and cut each slice into quarters, either into triangles or squares.

In a 1.5 litre (2½ pint) ovenproof dish, whisk the eggs, milk, sugar and vanilla together. Arrange the bread attractively in overlapping layers. Press down gently to immerse in the vanilla custard and leave to stand for 10 minutes.

Meanwhile, finely chop the ginger. Scatter it over the bread and finish by drizzling with half of the syrup.

Bake in the oven for 30–35 minutes until the top is golden and the custard is just set. Drizzle over the remaining syrup. Serve with plenty of cream to pour over.

# Plum and almond pudding (v.)

This one-dish pudding is incredibly delicious and very easy to make.

**Preparation time:**
15 minutes

**Cooking time:**
35 minutes

## Serves 6

150g (5oz) butter, plus
   extra for greasing
150g (5oz) caster sugar
3 eggs, beaten
150g (5oz) ground almonds
1 tsp baking powder
Finely grated zest of
   1 orange
3 tbsp orange juice
1 kg (2¼lb) plums,
   halved and stoned
1 tbsp flaked almonds
1 tbsp demerara sugar
1 tsp ground cinnamon

**To serve**
Cream or custard

Preheat the oven to 180°C (350°F), Gas Mark 4. Butter a a shallow ovenproof dish, about 1.5–2 litre (2½–3½ pint) capacity then place the butter and caster sugar into the dish, and using an electric mixer, whisk together until light and fluffy.

Fold in the eggs, ground almonds, baking powder and orange zest and juice until combined. Smooth the top.

Push the plums into the mixture being as neat or as random as you like. Scatter over the flaked almonds, demerara and cinnamon.

Bake in the oven for 35 minutes until risen and golden. Serve with plenty of cream or custard.

# Pear and chocolate pastries (v.)

These little tarts couldn't be easier to make, but guests always think I've made a complex dessert worthy of the finest French patisserie! I should take this recipe to my grave to avoid being discovered ... but here's to sharing it! If you can't find whole baby pears use jars or tins of whole baby figs, peaches or apricot halves. Alternatively, just make the pastries into rectangles and use tinned pear halves instead.

**Preparation time:**
20 minutes,
  plus chilling
**Cooking time:**
12–15 minutes

**Makes 6**

6 whole baby pears in
  syrup (available in jars)
375g (13oz) bought
  ready-rolled puff pastry
Plain flour, for dusting
6 tsp hazelnut chocolate
  spread

**To serve**
Cream

Strain the pears and reserve the syrup. Roll out the pastry on a lightly floured surface so that it's about half its original thickness. Using an 8cm (3in) cutter stamp out 12 circles, re-rolling the pastry if necessary.

Place 6 pastry circles onto a non-stick baking tray. Place a spoonful of chocolate spread into the centre of each one, ensuring there is a generous pastry border around each one.

Brush a little of the reserved pear syrup around the pastry edges to act as glue. Top with the remaining pastry, lining up the edges neatly, and pressing gently to remove any air, and seal the edges tightly.

Make a little indentation with your finger in the centre of each one – this will stop the pear from wobbling off! Sit a pear, stalk uppermost, onto the centre of each chocolate-filled cushion and push down gently to ensure it is secure. Cover lightly and place into the fridge for 1 hour or for up to 6 hours.

Preheat the oven to 200°C (400°F), Gas Mark 6. Brush lightly with some of the reserved syrup. Bake in the oven for 12–15 minutes or until the pastry border is risen and golden. Remove from the oven and immediately brush with more syrup to glaze. Serve hot with cream to pour over.

# Apricot and marzipan tart  (v.)

This super-simple pudding is ready in no time. For ultimate convenience, or out of season, use tinned apricots instead — you'll need about 10 halves.

**Preparation time:**
10 minutes
**Cooking time:**
15–20 minutes

### Serves 4

375g (13oz) bought
  ready-rolled puff pastry
175g (6oz) golden marzipan
400g (14oz) apricots,
  halved and stoned
1 tbsp caster sugar

**To serve**
Cream or ice cream

Preheat the oven to 200°C (400°F), Gas Mark 6. Unroll the pastry and place on a large non-stick baking sheet. Using the tip of a sharp knife, score around the pastry to make a 2cm (¾in) border. Prick the centre of the pastry all over with a fork.

Coarsely grate the marzipan and sprinkle it evenly over the central pastry rectangle, avoiding the scored line and border.

Arrange the apricots evenly over the top, cut side up, again avoiding the border. Sprinkle the sugar over the fruit.

Bake in the oven for 15–20 minutes or until the pastry border is risen and golden and the fruit is glazed and tender. Remove from the oven and leave to cool for 5 minutes before cutting into squares and serving with cream or ice cream.

# Under the Grill

# Chargrilled paprika chicken with corn and tomato salsa

This tasty one-tray recipe benefits from the extra flavour it gets from a good grilling! Serve with warmed flour tortillas.

**Preparation time:**
10 minutes

**Cooking time:**
20 minutes

**Serves 4**

4 x chicken breasts, skin on
2 whole sweet corn, papery skin removed
1 tbsp olive oil
½ tsp paprika
Finely grated zest and juice of ½ orange
1 tomato, diced
1 spring onion, trimmed and finely sliced
2 tbsp chopped fresh coriander
Sea salt and freshly ground black pepper

**To serve**
8–12 warmed flour tortillas

Preheat the grill to medium. Place the chicken and sweet corn into a grill pan large enough to take both in a single layer. Rub the chicken and sweet corn with the olive oil and paprika.

Cook for about 15 minutes, turning often, until the corn is tender. Remove the corn and set aside. Continue cooking the chicken for a further 5 minutes or until there is no pink meat and the skin is crispy.

When the corn is cool enough to handle, stand one of the cobs on its end on a board. Run a sharp knife from top to bottom around the central core to release the kernels. Discard the core. Repeat with the other cob.

Remove the chicken from the grill and drizzle over the orange juice. Add the corn kernels, tomato, spring onion, coriander and orange zest to the chicken. Mix well and season to taste. Divide between 4 warmed plates and serve with warmed flour tortillas.

# Caramelised onion and steak sandwiches

Sometimes the simple things are the best, and for me a steak sandwich is one of these. Coating the steaks in mustard before cooking gives the meat a great flavour and a bit of a twist too.

**Preparation time:**
5 minutes

**Cooking time:**
6–12 minutes

## Serves 2

2 small red onions, peeled
2 x 150g (5oz) thick rump
   or sirloin steaks
1 tbsp wholegrain mustard
1 tbsp olive oil
Sea salt and freshly
   ground black pepper
2 x 10–15cm (4–6in) pieces
   French bread, cut in half
2 tbsp houmous

**To serve**
A handful of rocket leaves
Sliced tomatoes

Line the grill pan with foil and set a rack over the top. Preheat the grill to medium or prepare a barbecue. Cut each onion into thick, horizontal slices.

Rub the steaks all over with mustard and drizzle with half of the olive oil. Rub the remaining oil over the onions. Season both with salt and pepper.

Place on the rack under the grill or on the barbecue and cook for 3–4 minutes on each side for rare, or longer until cooked to your liking, and the onions are caramelised and starting to char at the edges.

About 1 minute before the steak is cooked place the bread under the grill, cut side up, and cook until warm and golden. Spread the grilled bread with houmous, and top with the steak and onions. Serve with the rocket and tomato in the sandwich or on the side.

# Chimichurri pork burgers

Chimichurri is a blend of herbs, spices and onion originating from South America. It's traditionally served with beef steaks, but here it works really well with pork. However, if you'd rather be a little more traditional, use beef mince instead. These burgers are perfect for the grill or barbecue.

**Preparation time:**
15 minutes

**Cooking time:**
20 minutes

## Serves 4

100ml (4fl oz) olive oil
3 tbsp red wine vinegar
1 small onion, peeled and
  very finely chopped
2 garlic cloves, peeled
  and crushed
20g (¾oz) fresh flat leaf
  parsley, finely chopped
½ tsp dried oregano
½ tsp dried chilli flakes
1 tsp ground cumin
¼ tsp salt
500g (1lb 2 oz) pork mince
4 burger buns, split in half

**To serve**
Salad leaves
Soured cream

Whisk the olive oil and vinegar together. Add the onion, garlic, parsley, dried herbs, spices and salt. Mix well and reserve about 4 tablespoons of the mixture for later.

Line the grill pan with foil and set a rack over the top. Preheat the grill to medium or prepare a barbecue. Add the pork mince and mix really well – your hands are best for this job – until the pork is smooth.

With damp hands, shape the pork mixture into 4 large patties. Place onto the rack under the grill or on the barbecue and cook for 8–10 minutes on each side or until browned and there is no more pink meat in the centre.

Place the burger buns, cut-side up, under the grill for the last minute of cooking, until golden. Assemble the burgers on the buns with a bed of salad leaves. Drizzle over the reserved chimichurri, like a relish, and serve with soured cream on the side.

# Sticky five-spice pork

Eating sticky, gooey ribs with your hands is such a delight, but the ribs do need long cooking to become tender and tasty. Partly cooking the ribs without their sticky glaze ensures that they are cooked without being burnt to a cinder on the outside.

**Preparation time:**
5 minutes
**Cooking time:**
40–45 minutes,
  plus resting

**Serves 4**

850g (1lb 14oz) pork ribs
6 tbsp hoisin sauce
2 tbsp clear honey
2 tbsp dry sherry
2 tsp Chinese five-spice
  powder
2 tbsp soy sauce
1 tbsp vegetable oil

**To serve**
Crusty bread
Coleslaw

Preheat the grill to medium or prepare a barbecue. Place the ribs into a grill pan just large enough to hold the ribs in a single layer.

Pour over 500ml (18fl oz) boiling water from a kettle and cook under the grill or on the barbecue for 20–25 minutes, turning once, until the ribs are opaque.

Remove the pan from the grill and tip off any excess water. Leave the ribs to cool for 10 minutes. Stir the remaining ingredients into the tray, turning the ribs over to coat in the mixture. Return to the grill or onto the barbecue. Cook for 20 minutes, turning often, until sticky and browned.

Remove from the grill. Cover the tray with foil and leave to rest for 5 minutes. Serve just as they are or with coleslaw and crusty bread.

# Chunky vegetable and houmous wraps (v.)

These easy veggie wraps are really satisfying. Use the grilled veggies immediately while hot or leave to cool for assembling in the wraps later.

**Preparation time:**
10 minutes

**Cooking time:**
15 minutes,
   plus resting

**Serves 4**

1 red pepper, deseeded
1 yellow pepper, deseeded
1 large aubergine
2 courgettes
2 red onions, peeled
3 tbsp olive oil
Sea salt and freshly
   ground black pepper
1 tbsp red wine vinegar
A large pinch of dried
   mixed herbs
4 large flour wraps
4 tbsp houmous

Preheat the grill to medium-high. Cut the vegetables lengthways into batons and the onion into thin wedges. Place into a large grill tray. Drizzle over the olive oil and a generous amount of salt and pepper.

Grill for 15 minutes, turning occasionally, until softened and coloured. Switch off the grill. Drizzle over the vinegar, and sprinkle the herbs over the vegetables. Leave in the turned-off grill for 15 minutes.

Five minutes before the vegetables are ready, place the wraps onto one of the empty grill racks to warm through (even though the grill is switched off it will still be warm).

Spread the houmous over the wraps and top with the vegetables. Turn in the bottom edge of the wrap, and then roll up from the sides to enclose the filling. Eat immediately.

# Fish with golden Parmesan topping

The thought of cooking with mayonnaise triggers a bit of the food snob in me! But my Mum cooks a version of this dish and it tastes surprisingly sophisticated, and always leaves diners wondering what the secret ingredient is. So now you all know — sorry Mum.

**Preparation time:**
5 minutes

**Cooking time:**
7–10 minutes

**Serves 4**

A little butter, for greasing
4 x 150g (5oz) chunky white
   fish fillets, such as cod or
   haddock
Sea salt and freshly
   ground black pepper
3 tbsp good-quality
   mayonnaise
3 tbsp finely grated fresh
   Parmesan cheese

**To serve**
Crusty bread
Dressed green salad

Preheat the grill to high. Lightly butter the base of a flameproof baking dish.

Arrange the fish in the dish and cook under the grill for 2–3 minutes until just opaque.

Turn the fish over with a fish slice and season with a little salt and pepper. Spread the mayonnaise neatly over the fish fillets and sprinkle over the Parmesan.

Return to the grill and cook for a further 5 minutes or until the cheese is golden and bubbling, and the fish is opaque. Serve with crusty bread and a dressed green salad.

# Grilled halloumi and vegetable salad (v.)

Halloumi, or squeaky cheese as my god-daughter Floss calls it (due to the sound it makes when you bite into it), is a rather clever cheese. It can be grilled or fried, and will hold its shape. Oh, and it tastes good too.

**Preparation time:**
5 minutes

**Cooking time:**
20 minutes

**Serves 2**

1 small aubergine
1 courgette
1 red pepper, deseeded
12 cherry tomatoes
1 tbsp fresh oregano leaves
3 tbsp olive oil
Sea salt and freshly
   ground black pepper
225g (8oz) halloumi, cut
   into chunks
75g (3oz) baby spinach
   leaves
1 tbsp balsamic vinegar

**To serve**
Crusty bread

Preheat the grill to high. Cut the aubergine, courgette and red pepper into chunks.

Place into a large grill tray with the tomatoes, oregano and olive oil. Season generously and toss together to coat in the oil.

Grill for 20 minutes, turning regularly, until softened and browned, but not charred. Top with the halloumi and cook for a further 1–2 minutes until golden.

Remove the grill pan and add the spinach. Drizzle over the balsamic vinegar and season to taste. Toss well to combine. Serve warm with plenty of crusty bread.

# Grilled lime and chilli chicken

Chicken wings should be sticky but crispy in my book! That might sound like an impossible combination, but try this simple recipe and you'll find out what I mean.

**Preparation time:**
5 minutes,
 plus marinating
**Cooking time:**
25 minutes

**Serves 4**

8–12 chicken wings
Finely grated zest and
 juice of 2 limes
¼–½ tsp dried chilli flakes
2 tbsp olive oil
Sea salt and freshly
 ground black pepper

**To serve:**
Crusty bread
Salad or coleslaw

Place the chicken into a flameproof dish that's large enough to take it in a single layer. Add the finely grated zest and juice of the limes, chilli flakes and olive oil. Season generously.

Mix everything together to coat evenly. If you have time, cover and chill in the fridge for 1–12 hours, turning a couple of times. If not don't worry!

Preheat the grill to medium or prepare the barbecue. Cook the chicken in its dish for 25 minutes,
turning often, until crispy and cooked through – the juices should run clear when tested with the tip of a knife. Serve with crusty bread and salad or coleslaw.

# Grilled peach and pancetta salad

I came across this brilliant combination by accident when friends arrived unannounced and I had very little in the cupboards for them to snack on with drinks. In this recipe they are equally tasty, but more substantial as part of a salad.

**Preparation time:**
10 minutes

**Cooking time:**
15 minutes

## Serves 2

2 ripe peaches
4 thin slices of pancetta
100g (4oz) baby salad leaves
½ tbsp balsamic vinegar
1 tbsp extra virgin olive oil
Sea salt and freshly
   ground black pepper

**To serve:**
Crusty bread

Preheat the grill to high. Cut the unpeeled peaches into quarters and remove the stones.

Cut the pancetta in half lengthways. Wrap a piece around each peach quarter.

Place on a grill rack and cook for 5 minutes, turning once, until crisp and golden.

Pile the salad leaves onto plates and top with the crispy peaches. Drizzle with the balsamic vinegar and olive oil and season to taste. Serve with crusty bread.

# Hot salmon, fennel and lemon salad

This dish tastes fantastic and looks great too. It's also jolly good for us as the salmon is high in omega 3 and the olive oil is low in saturated fat.

**Preparation time:**
5–10 minutes

**Cooking time:**
10 minutes

**Serves 2**

1 lemon
2 x 150g (5oz) salmon fillets
Sea salt and freshly
  ground black pepper
1 fennel bulb, trimmed
1 tbsp olive oil
A handful (about 10g/⅓oz)
  of fresh flat-leaf parsley
  leaves

Line the grill pan with foil and set a rack over the top. Preheat the grill to medium. Cut half of the lemon into thin slices. Place the slices on the rack and top with the salmon skin side up. Season with salt and pepper.

Cook for 5 minutes on each side or until opaque and golden.

Meanwhile, slice the fennel very thinly. Mix with 1 tablespoon of the remaining lemon juice, the olive oil and parsley leaves. Season to taste.

Top with the salmon and drizzle with the remaining lemon juice. Serve with crusty bread.

# Middle Eastern lamb with chargrilled baba ganoush

This amazing lamb dish is perfect for the grill or barbecue. The lamb is rubbed with ras el hanout, which is a blend of spices used in Moroccan dishes. It's widely available in major supermarkets.

**Preparation time:**
10 minutes

**Cooking time:**
30–35 minutes, plus cooling

**Serves 6**

1.75kg (4lb) boneless rolled lamb shoulder
2 tbsp ras el hanout (Moroccan spice mix)
2 aubergines, about 300g (11oz) each
1 head garlic
About 8 large fresh mint leaves, roughly chopped
2 tbsp Greek yoghurt
Sea salt and freshly ground black pepper

Preheat the grill to high or prepare the barbecue. Unroll the lamb joint leaving just a flat 'butterflied' piece of meat of even thickness all over. Rub the ras el hanout all over the meat until it is completely covered.

Place the meat, whole aubergines and head of garlic on the grill or barbecue and cook for 20 minutes, turning the meat and vegetables regularly to prevent them from burning. Remove the aubergine and garlic and set aside. Continue cooking the lamb for a further 10 minutes or until cooked through. Remove the meat from the grill and leave to rest for 5 minutes in a warm place.

When the aubergines are cool enough to handle, cut them in half lengthways. Use a spoon to scoop out the flesh and discard the skins and stems. Roughly chop the aubergine flesh and place in a bowl.

Peel the garlic. Squeeze 2 of the cloves out onto a board. Roughly chop and add them to the aubergine together with the mint and yoghurt. Season generously to taste and mix well. Cut the lamb into slices and serve with the baba ganoush and the remaining garlic cloves to squeeze over.

# Indian lamb and mango chutney kebabs

**These flavour-packed kebabs are perfect for the grill or barbecue, and are extremely easy, as they are all cooked together in one long row of joined skewers.**

**Preparation time:**
5 minutes, plus marinating

**Cooking time:**
17–20 minutes, plus resting

**Serves 4**

3 x 200g (7oz) lamb neck fillets of a similar size and length
2 tbsp mild curry powder
3 tbsp smooth mango chutney, plus extra to serve
4 chapattis or naan breads
75g (3oz) baby spinach leaves
150g (5oz) natural yoghurt

Trim the whole lamb fillets of any excess fat. Place them in a large freezer bag with the curry powder, seal the top and toss to coat. Add the mango chutney to the bag, seal and massage into the meat with your hands. Leave in the fridge for at least 1 hour or for up to 12 hours.

Preheat the grill to medium or prepare a barbecue. Place the fillets side by side, on a board. Using 4 long metal skewers, skewer the fillets together about 2.5cm apart (the skewers should be at right angles to the direction of the meat).

Place the meat under the grill or on the barbecue and cook for 10 minutes on each side, until browned. Remove from the grill and leave to rest on a clean board for 5 minutes. Slice the meat between each skewer to separate the skewers.

While the meat is resting, place the chapattis or naans under the grill or on the barbecue for 1–2 minutes on each side until warm. Serve the skewers on the breads, with the spinach leaves, mango chutney and yoghurt spooned over.

# Mushroom, walnut and blue cheese burgers (v.)

Vegetarians often seem to miss out when it comes to juicy, meaty burgers. This yummy alternative is packed with everything but the meaty bit. Choose mushrooms, which are as deep and bowl-like as possible, so they hold the filling.

**Preparation time:**
5 minutes

**Cooking time:**
7–10 minutes

**Serves 4**

4 large portabello or
  field mushrooms
4 tsp olive oil
1 small garlic clove,
  peeled and crushed
20g (¾oz) baby spinach
  leaves, shredded
25g (1oz) walnuts,
  roughly chopped
75g (3oz) blue cheese,
  such as Stilton, cubed
  or crumbled
4 burger buns, split in half

**To serve**
Sliced tomato
Thin red onion slices

Line the grill pan with foil and set a rack over the top. Preheat the grill to high. Rub the mushrooms all over with olive oil and garlic.

Place on the rack, gill side up, and cook for 5 minutes until browned and starting to soften.

Fill the mushrooms with the spinach, walnuts and then the cheese.

Place the buns, cut side up, on the rack with the filled mushrooms. Cook for a further 2 minutes or until the cheese is melted and bubbling, and the buns are golden. Fill the hot buns with the 'burgers' and tomato and red onion slices before serving.

# Prawn and chorizo tapas

Prawns and chorizo are a fantastic combination, and frequently served together in tapas and other Spanish dishes. This recipe is very simple and yet tastes so good, especially with some fresh crusty bread to go alongside.

**Preparation time:**
10 minutes
**Cooking time:**
12 minutes

**Serves 4 as a starter or light meal**

400g (14oz) raw, unpeeled
  tiger prawns
200g (7oz) chorizo, peeled
  and cut into chunks
8 cherry tomatoes, halved
1 garlic clove, peeled
  and finely sliced
2 tbsp olive oil
3 tbsp dry Fino sherry
Sea salt and freshly
  ground black pepper
2 tbsp double cream or
  crème fraîche
1 tbsp finely chopped
  fresh parsley

**To serve**
Crusty bread

Preheat the grill to medium. Place the prawns, chorizo, tomatoes, garlic, olive oil and sherry into an attractive flameproof dish (large enough to take most of the ingredients in a single layer). Mix well and season with salt and pepper.

Place under the grill and cook for 8–10 minutes, stirring frequently to baste in the juices, until the prawns are pink and the chorizo is golden.

Stir in the cream or crème fraiche and grill for a further minute or until hot through.

Scatter over the parsley and take to the table. Serve with plenty of crusty bread to mop up the sauce, and finger bowls with warm water and slices of lemon for dipping your prawn-peeling digits!

# Simple tomato and caper bruschetta (v.)

**Bruschetta are such an easy, tasty option for a light, filling meal. I often make an uncooked tomato topping, but this warm version brings out lots of different flavours.**

**Preparation time:**
5 minutes

**Cooking time:**
8 minutes

**Serves 2 as a starter or light meal**

4 plum tomatoes
1 tbsp extra virgin olive oil
1 tbsp baby capers, rinsed and drained
A large pinch of caster sugar
Sea salt and freshly ground black pepper
4 thick slices ciabatta
½ garlic clove, peeled
8 large fresh basil leaves, finely shredded

**To serve**
Fresh Parmesan cheese
Balsamic vinegar, to taste

Preheat the grill to high. Halve the tomatoes lengthways and place, cut side up and in a single layer, into a flameproof dish. Drizzle with the olive oil and scatter over the capers, sugar and some salt and pepper.

Place under the grill and cook for 7–8 minutes until piping hot and starting to colour, but still holding their shape.

Meanwhile, grill the ciabatta slices for 1 minute on each side until golden. Rub with the cut side of the garlic.

Top the prepared bread with the hot tomatoes and any pan juices, and sprinkle over the basil. Serve with Parmesan to shave over and balsamic vinegar to taste.

# Southern-style bourbon ribs and chips

Part-cooking the ribs in a foil parcel prevents the sticky glaze from burning to a crisp before the ribs are cooked. It also means there's little or no washing up!

**Preparation time:**
10 minutes
**Cooking time:**
55 minutes

### Serves 4

1 kg (2¼lb) whole pork ribs
4 tbsp clear honey
1 tbsp Worcestershire sauce
2 tbsp tomato ketchup
1 tbsp bourbon
2 large potatoes, unpeeled
1 tbsp vegetable oil
Sea salt and freshly
  ground black pepper

**To serve**
Green salad

Preheat the grill to high or prepare a barbecue. Place the ribs on a large double layer of foil. Add the honey, Worcestershire sauce, ketchup and smother over the ribs. Drizzle over the bourbon. Enclose the ribs in the foil like a parcel and scrunch the seams together tightly. Place into a large grill pan (large enough to take the ribs and the potatoes in a single layer).

Grill or barbecue in the pan for 30 minutes, turning the foil parcel over halfway through cooking. During the last 5 minutes of cooking, cut the potatoes in half and then into 1cm (½in) thick wedges, and rub generously with the vegetable oil.

Carefully open up the foil parcel, leaving the ribs and any juices contained within the foil. Scatter the potato wedges to one side of the open parcel in the grill pan. Season both with salt and pepper.

Return the pan to the grill and cook the ribs and potatoes for a further 20–25 minutes, turning frequently, until the meat is sticky and browned, and the potatoes are golden and tender. Serve immediately with green salad.

# Duck and honey-glazed fig salad

A wonderful salad that is perfect as a light meal or starter. Radicchio is a deep red, bitter-tasting Italian leaf available from all major supermarkets. As the duck cooks, it will lose quite a lot of fat, so be sure to cook it over a grill pan, both for cleanliness, and to collect the precious fat, which is amazing for using another day when cooking roast potatoes.

**Preparation time:**
5 minutes
**Cooking time:**
15 minutes

**Serves 4 as a starter or light meal,
2 as a main course**

2 large duck breasts, skin on
Sea salt and freshly ground black pepper
6 small figs, halved lengthways
2 tbsp clear honey
2 heads of radicchio, washed
1 tbsp balsamic vinegar

**To serve**
Warmed crusty bread

Preheat the grill to high and place a rack over the grill pan. Place the duck onto the rack, fat side up and season with salt and pepper.

Place under the grill in a medium position (if the tray is too close to the grill element the fat in the duck could cause the grill to flare and ignite). Cook for 12 minutes until the duck is golden. Remove the duck and leave to rest on a board while you cook the figs. If the grill is very smoky then pour off the fat as this will be the cause, and return the tray to the grill.

Place the figs, cut side up, onto the rack. Drizzle with half of the honey. Return to the grill and cook for 3 minutes until glazed and just golden.

Finely shred the radicchio and divide between 4 plates. Thinly slice the duck. Top the lettuce with the duck and grilled figs, and drizzle over the remaining honey and the balsamic vinegar. Serve with warmed crusty bread on the side.

# Sweet chilli tuna burgers with lime mayo

I am addicted to sweet chilli sauce! It's so versatile, and its sweetness adds body, tang and a bit of a kick to all sorts of things — stews, soups and sauces. Here it works brilliantly as a sticky glaze.

**Preparation time:**
5 minutes

**Cooking time:**
6–8 minutes

**Serves 2**

2 x 150g (5oz) fresh tuna steaks, chilled
1 tbsp sweet chilli sauce
2 tbsp sesame seeds
3 tbsp mayonnaise
2 soft burger buns, split in half
25g (1oz) baby spinach leaves
1 lime, cut into wedges

Line the grill pan with foil and set a rack over the top. Preheat the grill to high. Rub the tuna with the sweet chilli sauce until evenly covered on both sides. Scatter over the sesame seeds to give an even coating on both sides.

Place on the rack and cook for 2 minutes until the seeds are golden and crisp. Turn the steaks over and repeat on the other side.

Spread half of the mayonnaise onto the burger buns. Top with the baby spinach, followed by the tuna steaks. Spoon on the remaining mayonnaise and drizzle over half of the lime juice before capping with the top of the bun. Serve with the remaining lime wedges on the side.

# Vietnamese coconut beef skewers

These probably should be Thai skewers as they are made using Thai curry paste, but I like to serve them in French bread (like an Asian steak sandwich), which puts them firmly into Vietnamese territory — in Vietnam fresh baguettes are sold everywhere, a wonderful legacy of the French occupation.

**Preparation time:**
10 minutes

**Cooking time:**
10 minutes

**Serves 4**

500g (1lb 2oz) trimmed
    rump steak
1 tbsp Thai red curry paste
A pinch of salt
3 tbsp coconut cream
2 tbsp desiccated coconut

**To serve**
4 pieces of French bread,
    the same length as the
    skewers
Fresh coriander, basil and
    mint leaves
1 lime, cut into wedges

Line the grill pan with foil and set a rack over the top. Preheat the grill to high or prepare a barbecue. Cut the steak into long thin strips. Rub thoroughly with the curry paste and the salt. Weave the strips onto 4 long metal skewers. To do this, put the tip of the skewer into the meat, move it down about 2cm (¾in), skewer another piece of meat, then move it down about 2cm (¾in) and continue all the way down the strip of meat. Continue until all the meat and skewers have been used up.

Using a pastry brush, brush a little of the coconut cream onto the meat.

Place under the grill or on the barbecue and cook for 4 minutes on each side, brushing every minute or so with more coconut cream, until browned and fragrant. Remove from the grill and sprinkle over the desiccated coconut to coat the meat completely.

Put each skewer between 2 pieces of bread and slide the meat off the skewers. Top with the fresh herbs and serve with lime wedges to squeeze over.

# Summer berry and white chocolate gratin (v.)

A quick dessert which tastes fantastic! The berries are a perfect contrast to the creamy mascarpone and rich white chocolate, which crisps up like a brûlée-style topping under the grill. If you prefer, make individual portions in flameproof ramekins.

**Preparation time:**
5 minutes

**Cooking time:**
8 minutes

**Serves 4**

400g (14oz) mixed
  summer berries, such
  as strawberries,
  blueberries, raspberries
1 orange
250g (9oz) mascarpone
50g (2oz) white chocolate

**To serve**
Shortbread biscuits

Preheat the grill to medium-low and position the shelf to low.

Place the fruit in a shallow layer in an 18 x 25cm (7 x 10in) ovenproof dish, cutting any larger berries into halves or quarters.

Finely grate the orange zest over the top and dot small spoonfuls of mascarpone neatly and evenly over the fruit so that it is completely covered.

Coarsely grate the chocolate evenly over the contents of the dish. Place under the grill and cook for about 7–8 minutes or until golden and bubbling – keep an eye on it as the chocolate can burn if the grill is too hot. Serve immediately with shortbread biscuits on the side.

# Caramelised bananas with pecan praline (v.)

This very easy recipe leaves the bananas coated in a crunchy caramel glaze with a tasty, brittle pecan praline to go alongside. Vanilla ice cream is a must to serve with this pudding — like a posh banana split.

**Preparation time:**
5 minutes

**Cooking time:**
3–5 minutes, plus resting

**Serves 4**

1 tsp vegetable oil
4 bananas
5 tbsp granulated sugar
25g (1oz) pecans, finely chopped

**To serve**
Lightly whipped cream or vanilla ice cream

Preheat the grill to high. Line a grill pan with foil and grease with the vegetable oil. Peel the bananas and cut them in half lengthways. Place cut side up on the foil with plenty of space between them.

Sprinkle liberally with the sugar so all the cut surfaces of the fruit and the surrounding foil is covered.

Place under the grill and cook for 3–5 minutes or until the sugar has become liquid and golden. Turn off the grill. Place the bananas onto serving plates and keep warm in the turned-off grill.

Meanwhile, set the grill pan and any remaining liquid caramel to one side and scatter over the pecans. Leave in a cool place for 3 minutes or until it becomes solid. Peel off the foil and break into shards. Scatter over the warm bananas. Serve with spoonfuls of lightly whipped cream or ice cream.

# Index

# Acknowledgements

I am indebted to Lizzy Gray, my editor, who has put her faith in me once again to produce this book. Lizzy you have been such a great support and mentor in the planning and writing of this, and all my other books, and I am so, so grateful to you. Thank you also to Helen Hawksfield who has taken this book from manuscript to printed matter with great patience and understanding; and to Kathy Steer who edited everything in such detail, and with super-speed! It's been wonderful to work with you all.

Thank you to the wonderful Jenny White who has made my food look so yummy in all the pictures. Jenny I can't believe I've known you and the girls for nearly five years already! It's been great to get to know you and the lovely Col, and I wish you much happiness for your future together as a family in your country pile!

Thank you too, Dan Jones, for your beautiful photographs. They're fab!

My life would be impossibly hard without my loyal friends, and my wonderful family. Mummy and Daddy, Simon and Sophie, I thank you for all your love, support, care and understanding; and for your endless ability to make everything alright, and then make everything better than alright, no matter what life brings.

As for my darling Rupert – this year has been the best of my life so far, and I have you to thank for it. Thank you so much for being utterly brilliant. Here's to plenty more of the same in the years we share together in the future.

# About the Author

Katie Bishop is a successful food writer and stylist. Her love of food led her to enter the acclaimed Young Cook of Britain competition at the age of 14. Katie beat over 32,000 entrants to win, giving her the opportunity to work alongside some of Britain's most renowned chefs.

Katie has worked as a chef around the world but is now based in London. She regularly writes for food magazines, contributes to online sites, pens bestselling cookbooks and appears as a guest chef on TV.